# Whitetail
# Rites of Autumn

Text and Photography by

## Charles J. Alsheimer

Published by

**kp krause publications**
An F&W Publications Company

**700 East State Street • Iola, WI 54990-0001**
**715-445-2214 • 888-457-2873**
**www.krause.com**

To place an order or obtain a free catalog, please call 800-258-0929.

Library of Congress Catalog Number 2003108897
ISBN 0-87349-534-9

Editor—Joel Marvin

Printed in China.

# Dedication

For Paul H. Daniels, Jr.

To my country neighbor, close friend, photography assistant, and in many
ways the brother I never had, I say thanks for the memories.

# Table of Contents

# F o r e w o r d

I became a friend of Charlie Alsheimer years before we ever shook hands. The friendship was a little one-sided in that he didn't have a clue who I was, but I sure knew Charlie was my buddy.

You see, Charlie talked to me every month through the pages of *Deer & Deer Hunting* magazine. He spoke to me about hunting white-tailed deer in a language I understood and related to. Charlie was different from the other outdoor writers. When I read his articles, it was as though he and I were right there together setting up a treestand or watching a buck make a scrape. His words and photos touched me unlike those of any other writer or photographer. It was clear that Charlie and I were always on the same page when it came to deer hunting.

Over the years I have come to realize that Charlie Alsheimer has thousands of friends just like me. In my travels across the U.S., I have met scores of whitetail enthusiasts who identify Charlie as the outdoor communicator who most consistently writes about things they can identify with and know to be real. If you don't believe me, ask any of the editors Charlie has worked for, and you will hear the same comments over and over again. Charlie's writing connects with his readers. He understands deer and he understands deer hunters.

Because of this, readers of *Whitetail Rites of Autumn* are in for a treat. Not only does Charlie provide unparalleled insights into deer behavior, he also shares the personal side of his relationship with the whitetail. He describes in fascinating detail how he came to know and bond with the first buck (aptly named Charlie) he studied and photographed extensively. Ultimately, he shares the emotion he felt when the buck finally died.

Any expert will tell you that successful photographers have at least one thing in common – they are keen observers of their subject matter. After viewing this book, there is no question that Charlie is an especially keen observer of the whitetail. How else could he trip the shutter at just the right time to get the photo he was looking for? How else could he portray deer behavior with such clarity and insight? How else could he have become the best of the best at what he does?

*Whitetail Rites of Autumn* is a wonderful showcase for Charlie's talent as a deer observer, researcher and photographer. The book's chapters bring the whitetail's world to life, season by season. Its title is well-deserved, thanks to an incredibly detailed look at deer behavior during the fall months. Those who long for the time when acorns drop to the forest floor, leaves scream crimson, and fresh rubs appear overnight will undoubtedly enjoy this section. It's a great read on a winter night when you want to return to the woods to recapture that special moment you experienced last autumn, or the autumn before, or the one when you were a kid, or … well, you get the point.

Charlie and I finally shook hands in 1991. Since then, we have become close friends and I have learned a great deal from him. The time I spend with Charlie is very special to me, and *Whitetail Rites of Autumn* is a chance to spend even more time with him in an indirect way. I'll open it when I haven't talked to him for a couple of days and need my weekly whitetail fix. I'll open it when I'm thinking about how much his friendship means to me. Most of all, I'll open it when I'm feeling disconnected and want to go home to my mountain, to my deer, to my food plots, to the things I value most in life. Through his photography and writing, Charlie always takes me back to nature, and I'm sure he'll do the same for you.

Enjoy the trip.

Craig Dougherty
Vice Chairman, Fred Bear Equipment Company
Founder, North Country Whitetails
www.NorthCountryWhitetails.com

# Acknowledgments

Acknowledgments are never easy. If I attempted to thank everyone who has helped me over the years with my "whitetail pursuit," there would be page after page of thank you comments.

As with all my books, the concept for this book has been a lifetime in the making. Throughout my life, I've been blessed to know many wonderful people who have made my journey possible. To all, I'm deeply grateful. However, there have been a few who truly helped me chase my dream of being a full-time outdoor writer and photographer. Without them, this book would never have been possible.

First, I'd like to thank my dad for introducing me to the whitetail 50 years ago. He's gone now, but the time we spent chasing whitetails on our farm was the springboard for my career in the out-of-doors.

Next, I'd like to thank my wife, Carla. I've got the greatest woman in the world with which to share my life. In spite of a career of her own, she has always been there when I needed her. Thanks for being a wonderful wife and my best friend.

I offer a special thanks to my son, Aaron, for all he's done for me over the last 26 years. He's one of the best editors in the business and in many ways helped make this book what it is. From the Everglades to Alaska we've traveled in search of one more great photo. It didn't always happen, but we gave it our best shot.

To Haas Hargrave, I say thanks. Haas had a storied career as a WWII bomber pilot, college football coach and an outstanding businessman. He was my first boss out of college. He encouraged me to pursue a career in the outdoor field when others said it was financially impossible. He birthed a dream that became a reality.

I'm also indebted to *Deer and Deer Hunting* magazine founders Al Hofacker and Jack Brauer. These two stuck their neck out and gave me my first break in this business. Thank you both.

A special thanks is in order for past *Deer and Deer Hunting* editor Pat Durkin. During Pat's tenure as DDH editor, he provided me with many wonderful opportunities to grow. For this I'm thankful.

And to current *Deer and Deer Hunting* editor Dan Schmidt, I say thanks. We have a special chemistry when it comes to the white-tailed deer and the way we work together. It's a joy to work with and for you.

To Bob and Alma Avery: Thanks for loving me and allowing me to be a part of your family. You have one of the most incredible whitetail paradises on earth, and I appreciated you allowing me to photograph on your mountain spread.

To Ben Lingle: Thanks for giving me one of my first photography breaks. Access to your estate gave me some incredible insights into the world of the white-tailed deer.

Terry Rice: Thanks for all the help you've provided. Without you, some of these photos would not have been possible. You're a special friend.

Wayne Laroche: Thanks for turning on my lunar light bulb nearly 10 years ago. You're the most down-to-earth, common-sense wildlife biologist I've ever met. Your way of making the complex understandable never ceases to amaze me. You've been a great coach.

A special thanks is in order for my country friends and associates, Craig and Neil Dougherty. Along the way we've done a lot of whitetail brainstorming. Thanks for all the fireside chats. You are truly kindred spirits.

Jim, Charlie, Jack, Aaron, Paul, Whitey, Spook, Chucky, Carla and Buttercup: Without you I wouldn't have learned what I know about whitetails. Collectively you have taught me more than all the wildlife biologists or scientific journals combined. Thanks for providing me a window into the whitetail's hidden world.

And most importantly I want to thank Jesus Christ for my incredible blessings. He's provided me with health, the privilege of living in the greatest country on earth and having a dream job. His guidance and direction have made this book possible.

# Introduction

My roots run deep in the soil of western New York. Nearly 56 years ago, I was born into a family of potato farmers. My dad, Charles H. Alsheimer, was a rugged individual and a farmer to the core. He also was a deer hunter who was more than willing to share his love for whitetails with his only son. My introduction to the world of the whitetail came shortly after my fifth birthday while dad was checking the crops on our farm. He found a newborn fawn, and I can remember him letting me pet it as it lay in the grass. Then, later that fall, a big buck bounded in front of our pickup truck as we were checking the potato harvest. These two experiences were the beginning of my pursuit of the whitetail, a journey that has spanned half a century. It's hard to believe they took place so long ago because it seems like they occurred just yesterday.

"Seasons come and seasons go" are the words to a popular song. As I look back on my life, I realize that I've been blessed with many great seasons that were special in large part because of my relationship with the white-tailed deer. My early encounters with the whitetail caused me to not only fall in love with it, but also dream of building a career around it.

For the first 30 years of my life, I pursued the whitetail as an "amateur." During this time, I was content to observe, photograph and hunt this great animal on and around our farm in western New York State. In 1979, my relationship with the whitetail changed. The time I had spent in Vietnam a decade earlier had changed my outlook on life and motivated me to chase my dreams. Consequently, I decided to leave a career in sales and marketing to pursue my goal of becoming an outdoor writer and nature photographer. Though the career move was a bit suspect in the beginning, it has paid off in ways I never imagined.

During the last quarter century, my appreciation and respect for God's incredible creation has grown immensely. The experiences I've had as a photographer can only be described as "scripted in heaven." I've pursued elk in the Canadian Rockies and moose and grizzlies in Alaska's Denali National Park. I've photographed some of the most breathtaking stretches of scenery in North America, from the Everglades to the Arctic. In all my travels, though, I've never encountered any aspect of the natural world that captivates me like the whitetail. *Odocoileus virginianus* is the most incredible creature I've studied and photographed, and it has taught me so much about the wonders of God.

Over the years, I've been privileged to observe, photograph and hunt the whitetail in various regions throughout the United States and Canada. Along the way, I've taken nearly a million photos, and as you will see in this book, many of the behaviors I've photographed are quite unusual. My professional background is not as a biologist, though I've studied the whitetail's biology extensively. Some have said that my specialty is deer behavior, and I tend to agree with them. Though I continue to learn more all the time, I've witnessed nearly every behavior exhibited by the whitetail.

My farming background taught me the importance of managing the land's resources, one of which is the whitetail. Therefore, I'm a staunch believer in the stewardship command set forth in Genesis 2:15 (NIV): "The Lord God took the man and put him in the Garden of Eden to work it and take care of it." I make no apologies for the fact that I gained my knowledge and love of the whitetail through hunting, which I continue to do to this day. Although most of my work is done with a camera, photography really is an extension of my background as a hunter. Hunting is a scientifically sound management tool and the most efficient method known to man for stewarding and controlling the whitetail population. It helps keep the deer herd in balance with the range's carrying capacity, ensuring that the delicate balance of nature is not disrupted or damaged.

Using a variety of methods, I've sought to learn as much as possible about the white-tailed deer. Over 10 years ago, I began raising whitetails, not for hunting but rather to conduct behavioral research. In the process, I've been able to document and film many seldom-seen aspects of deer behavior. The *Day in the Life* sections of Chapters 9, 10 and 11 are intended to show what it's like to be a whitetail, and each segment is based on my past observations in the field. It has been exciting, enlightening and fulfilling to be involved in many cutting-edge studies on deer behavior. Chapter 8, *Touched by Light*, is one example of a research project in which I've been involved.

A lifetime of living and working with whitetails has given me a great appreciation for their personalities. I've come to realize that each animal has its own unique characteristics and is "fearfully and wonderfully made." Few people have studied individual personality differences in deer, though I'm sure more will do so in the future. My introduction to this fascinating side of the whitetail came by accident in 1986 while photographing on a large estate that did not allow hunting.

One day, while baiting deer around my photo blind, I discovered a button buck staring at me from 30 yards away. Our eyes locked and I figured he'd run at any moment. When he didn't, I tossed him some corn to see what he'd do. To make a long story short, I was able to get this buck and several other deer to "imprint" on the sound of shelled corn rattling around in a plastic can. If I shook the can, the deer would tolerate my presence.

Interestingly, that button buck lived to be 9 years old. Over those years, he allowed me to follow him wherever he went as long as I had food with me. As a result, I was able to capture on film numerous aspects of whitetail behavior, some of which biologists were not aware of previously.

Since 1986, I have used the same imprinting technique at an estate in Pennsylvania, deer wintering areas in New York's Adirondack Mountains, a ranch in Texas, and here on our farm. Actually, the technique is nothing new. Pavlov was the first to get a conditioned response from animals, and over the last 20 years, the same principle has allowed me to see the whitetail in a whole new way.

A good example of what a photographer can accomplish with an imprinted buck can be seen in Chapter 14, *Cast to Cast*. This buck lived on a very large and beautiful property that was off limits to hunting. When it was a year and a half old, I was able to imprint it with the aid of corn and apples. Because of this, the yearlong photo sequence was possible.

In terms of size and format, this project is similar to my book *Whitetail: Behavior Through the Seasons*, which was published in 1996. However, the similarities end there. The text and photos in this book are entirely different. In fact, most of the photos had not yet been taken when *Behavior Through the Seasons* was released. Because of the whitetail's complexity, I continue to learn new things about it all the time. Consequently, I've been able to build upon what I shared in *Behavior*.

The last 25 years have turned into an incredible journey—one I never expected when it began. During this time, I've been able to peer inside the whitetail's world, gaining a better understanding of this magnificent animal. As a result, the following pages will allow you to witness aspects of its life that are seldom seen.

When you have read the last word and looked at the final photo, I hope your admiration for the whitetail mirrors mine. In my opinion, this creature simply is the crown jewel of North American wildlife. Enjoy your journey through this book.

Charles J. Alsheimer • Bath, New York • January 28, 2003

# About the Author

Charles Alsheimer is an outdoor writer, lecturer, whitetail consultant and award-winning writer and nature photographer from Bath, N.Y. Alsheimer was born and raised on a farm and has devoted his life to photographing, writing and lecturing about the wonders of God's creation. Alsheimer specializes in white-tailed deer.

He is the northern field editor for *Deer and Deer Hunting* magazine and a contributing editor for *Whitetail News*. In the past 25 years, Alsheimer's work has taken him across North America. His photos have won many state and national contests, and his articles and photographs have appeared in nearly every major outdoor publication including *Outdoor Life, Field & Stream, Sports Afield*, Harris Publications and *Deer and Deer Hunting*. In addition he has written four popular books on the whitetail and co-authored a fifth. Alsheimer also owns and operates a white-tailed deer research facility and provides consulting services to various segments of the whitetail industry.

In a national poll conducted in January 2000 by *Deer and Deer Hunting*, Alsheimer was honored as one of deer hunting's top five inspirational leaders of the past century. The ballot included nearly 60 scientists, manufacturers, politicians, celebrities, communicators and hunters whose names are intertwined with deer hunting. Each had some way increased America's understanding of the white-tailed deer, whether through the invention of camouflage patterns, the establishment of national forest or the writing of internationally known books. Alsheimer ranked third behind Fred Bear and Aldo Leopold, and ahead of fourth-place finisher Teddy Roosevelt. This honor illustrates the respect Alsheimer has among deer hunters.

Alsheimer is an active member of the Outdoor Writers Association of America, the New York State Outdoor Writers Association and a life member of the National Rifle Association. He has also served as a nature photography instructor for the National Wildlife Federation at its Blue Ridge, Maine and Nova Scotia Summits.

Alsheimer lives with his wife on their farm in rural upstate New York. Additional information about him and his work can be found on his website, www.CharlesAlsheimer.com

# CHAPTER 1

# Autumn's Splendor

The seasons, ever changing, never ending. The beauty of living in the North is being able to see each season. Spring, summer, autumn and winter blend so beautifully into one another. The sights and smells of each are incredible.

The rebirth of spring brings a sense of newness. The long days and warmth of summer offer tranquility. Autumn is nature's grandest season, with its display of every color in the rainbow. The transformation that takes place during September and October just begs to be explored and taken in.

Then, on autumn's heels, comes winter, often referred to as nature's locking time. Winter is certainly a season of beauty, but in the North it's also very harsh. In many ways, it's the vehicle nature uses to purge its old and weak.

The bonus that comes with each season is the wildlife—God's living, breathing gift for man to enjoy and utilize. Of all the wildlife God created, the white-tailed deer is perhaps the grandest of all. And no season showcases the whitetail's grandeur more than autumn.

# The Lure

For over 30 years I've had a passion for capturing the wonders of nature on film. Though I love photographing every season, autumn is my favorite. It truly is one of the joys of my life.

I've lived my whole life in the North—the farm country of western New York, to be exact. During this time I've watched over 50 autumns come and go. Each has been a little different, but all have been beautiful. My affection for this season began as a youngster, growing up on a potato farm. For farmers, autumn is the final chapter of the year's labors—a payday of sorts. It's the reaping time, a time to cash in the efforts put forth during the other seasons.

No season tweaks our senses quite like autumn. Science tells us that 80 percent of learning comes through seeing. The sights of autumn are so incredible that we can't help but learn from what we see. The tapestry of red and gold colors painted on a hillside, the sight of the first hard frost of the year, and the smell of freshly fallen leaves on the forest floor are breathtaking. Truly, the smells and colors of this season are nothing short of sensory overload. In addition to scenic beauty, many other aspects of this season help make it such a grand spectacle. One of the biggest is wildlife.

Autumn would not be the same without the chorus of migrating Canada geese honking in the sky above or the scolding cry of blue jays on a cold, clear morning. The yelping calls made by a flock of turkeys as they search the forest floor for acorns and the thunderous wing beats of a flushing ruffed grouse are other examples of the

*The white-tailed deer is considered by many to be the crown jewel of North American wildlife. Its numbers surpass 30 million and is found from Central America to Canada.*

enhancing effect wildlife have on this season. But it's perhaps the white-tailed deer that defines and reveals the splendor of autumn better than any other wild creature.

For millions of American sportsmen, the whitetail is the animal that causes them to pause, ponder and appreciate the beauty of this special season. As I grew through my teen years, a passion for deer hunting led me to spend untold hours exploring the wild haunts of our farm. As a result, I was introduced to the myriad wonders of nature. It's safe to say that I probably never would have learned to appreciate frosty mornings,

milkweed seed floating on autumn thermals, or acorns ricocheting off the forest floor if my pursuit of the whitetail hadn't introduced me to these finer points of the season. Sitting in a deer-stand on a cold morning as the sun creeps over the horizon can teach one a lot about nature.

I've also realized that time spent in an autumn forest has a way of revealing life's journey. Every time I see a brightly colored leaf floating to the forest floor, I think of the life it's had—from a bud in spring, to full growth in summer, to its death in autumn. Its journey is kind of like our trek through life.

It has been said that passions come and go, and I guess my passion for photography could have waned had it not been for the whitetail. This animal has kept my photography and writing career fresh. The residual benefits I've received from pursuing whitetails have inspired me to photograph all of nature, not just deer. Consequently, the experiences I've had with the whitetail have enriched my life beyond measure.

## Enriching Encounter

In many ways, I grew up with the white-tailed deer. As a farm kid, I saw deer on a daily basis. Though these experiences laid the groundwork for my career, it was a chance encounter with a whitetail that enabled me to learn so much about this incredible creature.

Though my appreciation for nature was formed as a child, it wasn't until I became a serious photographer that I realized how awesome God's creation is. For over three decades I've explored North America with a 35mm camera, trying to capture each special moment. My career has been a blessing and an eye opener.

In the fall of 1986, I discovered a side of whitetails that enabled me to truly get "up close and personal" with certain deer. I had gained permission to photograph on a large piece of unhunted land in the Adirondack Mountains of northern New York. My goal was to attempt to photograph the property's deer when they came to the feeding area at the end of each day. After several days of mediocre photography, I caught a break that literally changed my life.

While replenishing the bait around my photo blind, I discovered a button buck staring at me from 30 yards away. I was surprised because all the other deer had spooked when they saw me, but this one didn't. Our eyes locked and I figured he'd run at any moment. When he didn't, I tossed him some corn to see what he'd do. Instead of running, the young buck remained calm and started to eat.

From this point on, every time I returned to photograph, I'd rattle the corn can and the deer would eventually show up. The family that owned the property began calling the buck "Charlie" because of how we interacted with each other.

For the next nine years I returned to the area on a regular basis to photograph. During this time, Charlie and I forged an incredible relationship. As long as I had the "can of corn," he usually provided a window into his world.

*Top:* Between September 1 and October 1 the whitetail buck's testosterone level nearly doubles. With their hormone level beginning to flow at a fever pitch, bucks will begin expanding their territories. **Bottom:** Soon after peeling velvet in September, bucks begin making rubs throughout their territory. Rubs are a visual and scent "fingerprint" for each buck.

Over the course of his life, I spent hundreds of hours following him around his home area in the rural confines of the Adirondacks. To give you an idea of what our relationship was like, I'll share from some of my notes.

"October 13, 1989: Clear, heavy frost—beech trees in full autumn color. What an unbelievable morning! I arrived at the feeding area at dawn with hopes of photographing deer before they bedded for the day. As the sun inched over Ram Pasture Mountain, I spotted Charlie making his way out of the beaver flow, two hundred yards away. I hurried down the old logging road, trying to get his attention by rattling my corn can as I went. He heard me coming and in an instant shifted gears and headed toward me. After feeding on my scattered corn for a few minutes, he turned and headed up the forested hillside. I followed at a distance.

For the better part of an hour, Charlie walked slowly up the steep hill, stopping occasionally to make a scrape and eat fallen cherry leaves. Twice he encountered does, but didn't pursue them as they bounded away. Near the hill's summit, the big buck walked into a tangle of low-growing hemlocks and bedded. To get a better view, I continued to climb above him before sitting down on a large rock outcropping. From my vantage point twenty yards away, only the tips of his antlers were visible above the hemlock boughs.

For the next three hours I sat on the rock, taking in all that autumn was throwing at me. I was mesmerized by the rays of the early-morning sun dancing off the west branch of the Sacandaga River below. An hour into my watch the wind picked up and falling leaves began raining down on every inch of forest within sight. What a leaf storm! What an experience!

The three hours ended on an abrupt note. Before I knew what was happening, Charlie began staring back in my direction. For a minute I thought he was trying to say, 'Hey, buddy, throw me a little corn, will ya?' Eventually I realized he was looking past me. Slowly I turned around. Forty yards behind me, a coyote stood motionless. In one motion Charlie exploded from his bed and vanished down the steep hill into a sea of hemlock growth, while the coyote ran away from me in the opposite direction.

For a few moments I sat alone, taking it all in before heading off the hill and back to my car."

During the span of our nine years together I was able to photograph nearly every behavior a whitetail buck exhibits during the course of its life. Few things escaped my camera as I recorded the interaction between Charlie and the other deer in the area. Not only was I able to photograph some incredible fights, but I also chronicled interesting rutting behavior like scraping and rubbing, as well as various forms of interaction between bucks and does. As a result, I was able to gain insight into the whitetail's world that few have experienced.

In addition to Charlie, I "imprinted" five other deer from the area on the sound of shelled corn rattling around in a plastic can. As amazing as it sounds, I was able to get these deer to tolerate my presence simply by shaking the can.

In the end, Charlie wasn't a majestic buck, but he wore the scars of his nine years well. He eluded predators, endured incredible buck fights, and survived the brutal northern winters before dying of natural causes. Instead of letting coyotes and crows pick his body clean, I buried him beside a small stream similar to the one where we met on a cool autumn evening nine years before. Although it seems like a fairy tale, the bond he and I formed was a true love story, one that probably will never be repeated in nature.

It was partly because of autumn that we first met, and it was in autumn that our journey together came to an end as I buried him. By virtue of the fall seasons we spent together,

*By the time Autumn's colors have arrived, a doe's fawns will have lost their spots and be fat and sleek-looking.*

I gained a greater appreciation for whitetails and the rest of nature as well. It's hard to think that a deer could touch a soul, but Charlie did in so many ways.

## The Best Is Yet To Come

In the coming chapters, I'll share what I've learned during my 50-plus years in the deer woods. I feel very fortunate to have had so many wonderful experiences. Though there have been trials occasionally, the time I have spent pursuing the whitetail has brought blessings beyond measure.

*Whitetail Rites of Autumn* chronicles a journey that begins long before the leaves change their colors and fall from the trees. In my mind, it starts in the spring, when antlers begin growing and the North's landscape is reborn after emerging from a blanket of snow.

# CHAPTER 2

# Prelude to Autumn – Spring

Autumn may be the crown jewel of the seasons, but spring is a close second. What springtime lacks in color variation, it more than makes up for with the emotions it exudes. It's the season of rebirth for all of nature—a magical transition from dormancy to life. This is especially evident in the North. In regions where heavy snowfall is common, the harshness of winter often makes one wonder if better days will ever come.

By the time spring arrives, whitetails in many northern regions are teetering on the edge of collapse. Most have survived January, February and March on very little food. Just when it appears that winter will deliver the whitetail its deathblow, spring comes to the rescue.

The bloom of springtime is a wonder in itself, not to mention a Godsend to the whitetail. The short days of winter gradually increase in length, the earth warms, and whitetails become more active.

As March gives way to April, the sun shines brighter and the air isn't as cold. On south-facing hillsides throughout whitetail country, tender green shoots and the first wildflowers sprout forth. With their arrival, whitetails become more active, gorging themselves on the new growth.

# Food

During the winter months, the whitetail's food requirement lessens. In some cases, deer may go days without eating if the weather is extremely harsh. This changes with the arrival of spring green-up. With the lush new growth, whitetails seem to play catch-up by feeding throughout the day. Contrary to popular belief, they are very selective feeders and will not eat all new growth.

During 2001, with the assistance of North Country Whitetails and Cornell University's NEAS Lab, I conducted a browse analysis with the deer in our western New York research facility. We discovered that, in many cases, plants with high-protein levels are not always preferred deer food.

After consulting with animal nutritionists, the assumption was reached that a plant's digestibility, sugar level and nutrient content all play parts in determining which vegetation deer prefer. If available, whitetails will consume a balance of grasses, wildflowers, mushrooms, lichens, fruits (wild strawberries), nuts (leftover acorns and beechnuts), leaves, twigs and shrubs in the springtime. The volume of food consumed depends on the age and size of the animal, but in many cases whitetails can be expected to eat 10 or more pounds of highly nutritious food during this time of year.

Plants are nothing more than the delivery mechanism for the nutrients in the soil. Therefore, soils play a big role in the nutritional content of whitetail forage. Many animal nutritionists feel that if the soil in an area is poor and has a pH so low that it cannot produce springtime deer foods with at least 8 percent protein, the overall health of the deer herd will suffer.

## Physical Condition

By the time whitetails emerge from the ravages of winter, many will be strikingly thin. Their fur will often appear scruffy or blotchy. To the unknowing public, such an appearance is often cause for alarm. In reality, it's part of the annual cycle known as molting. This is nothing more than the hair in a deer's winter coat falling out as it gives way to the summer coat.

Fighting scars can be easily seen on both bucks and does when the molting process begins. Such scars often appear to be pink in color but change to a darker tone as the summer coat starts to grow in.

Of all the seasons, a whitetail's appearance is least attractive during spring. Their rather pitiful appearance at this time of the year is a far cry from the sleek, majestic-looking animals they become in summer, fall, and early winter.

*By the time spring green-up arrives, whitetails feed heavily on the lush green forage. This doe (center) is near the end of her gestation cycle and is accompanied by her offspring from the previous year.*

*When leaf-out occurs, all whitetails gravitate to the nutritious new growth. The new leaves on some tree species can have a protein level exceeding 10 percent.*

food is available, bucks and does will usually cover less than 1000 acres during springtime.

## Buck Behavior

Sex segregation within the whitetail population is a behavior that always has been fascinating to me. It's particularly evident during spring and summer. Once spring arrives, does form their own family groups and bucks form bachelor groups. Aside from using common feeding areas like clover and alfalfa fields, these two groups tend to keep to themselves. Though researchers have documented that bachelor groups can vary in size from two to 15 animals (or more), they typically include two to six bucks.

*Hierarchy:* A buck's bachelor group behavior can be very interesting during the spring. In farm country, it's common for bucks to know each other from previous interaction. Because of this, a dominance hierarchy develops within bachelor groups long before autumn's rut. Though not always the case, the older, aggressive bucks will generally be the "leaders of the pack." Occasionally, I've seen younger, more aggressive

## Home Range

During the winter months, a whitetail will not cover a great deal of ground; in many cases, its territory will consist of less than 1000 acres, providing food is available. However, when spring green-up arrives, deer begin to disperse to the ancestral range they inhabit during spring, summer and fall. In some cases, this is a trek of 20 miles or more. The speed of a whitetail's spring migration often depends on a host of factors, with the availability of food being one of the most significant. In the western New York farm country where I live, deer seldom travel more than 4 miles after winter's end. If lush, nutritious

*By mid-May, a mature buck's antlers are over 3 inches long. As the daylight increases, antler growth will accelerate. During the peak of the antler-growing process, mature bucks have been known to grow their antlers between ¼ and 1 inch a day.*

bucks dominate older, larger bodied males in spring and summer.

During this time, fights often break out among bucks. Because they either have yet to begin growing antlers or are in the early stages of antler growth, these fights usually involve two bucks standing on their hind legs, boxing or flailing with their hooves. With antler growth minimal and testosterone levels at low ebb, dominant bucks can keep subordinate deer in line with little more than an eardrop, a hard look or a snort-wheeze vocalization.

**Signposting:** Although signposting is commonly viewed as an autumn behavior, bucks use various forms of it during the spring and summer. However, it is much less intense at this time of the year. Researchers have identified at least six areas of a whitetail's body that have specialized glandular

*Where the whitetail population does not exceed its range's carrying capacity, wildflowers, like this Columbine, will be prevalent.*

tissues that emit scent. The whitetail's tarsal, preorbital, forehead and nasal glands are commonly used by bucks to communicate with one another.

Whitetails often will use a scrape's overhanging licking branch to deposit scent year-round. This is especially true of scrapes located in prime travel corridors. When a buck works a licking branch in the spring, he'll do so in much the same way he did in the fall. In the process he'll rub his nasal, preorbital and forehead glands on the branch, and salivate on it as well. Such behavior telegraphs his presence to all deer in the area. On occasion, bucks also will urinate into a scrape during the springtime period. I've even seen them paw at the ground during the spring, though this is rare. It's been my experience that spring signposting generally is confined to scent being deposited on a scrape's overhanging licking branch or on branches in a travel corridor.

## Antler Growth

Antlers are the fastest growing bone material known to man. Hormones control the cycle of antler growth—growing, hardening and casting. Increasing day length, or photoperiod, is responsible for triggering and regulating the antler growth process.

Over the years I've raised a few bucks that didn't drop their antlers until April 1. However, mature bucks that complete the casting process between December and March will usually begin to show antler growth by the end of March. The antler growing process will continue until about the first part of August in the North. Unlike mature bucks, yearlings normally do not begin growing their first antlers until late April or early May.

Antlers are an outgrowth of bone from the pedicles located at the top of a buck's skull. Growth occurs at the tips of antlers, which are

*This fawn is less than an hour old. Within the first 24 hours, the fawn will imprint on the doe and obey its every command for the next 2 months.*

quite soft and easily damaged during the early stages of their development. During springtime, the new antler growth consists primarily of cartilage material surrounded by sensory nerves and blood vessels that carry blood to the fast-growing antlers. The outer coating of the antler is covered with a velvet-like skin layer. Scientists believe that the hairs on the velvet serve as touch-sensitive feelers that help to prevent deer from damaging the antlers as they grow.

During the 120-day antler-development period, the growth rate of a buck's rack can be quite impressive if the animal is healthy and highly nutritious foods are available. In some cases, it's not uncommon for a buck's antlers to grow anywhere from ¼ inch to 1 inch of bone a day. On bucks that sport trophy-size antlers, the growth rate can be even greater than this.

## Doe Behavior

During the early part of spring, does stay away from bucks for the most part, choosing instead to live within their own family groups on range that is familiar to them. A doe family group normally consists of the oldest doe, her offspring from the previous year, daughters, and possibly granddaughters.

During the latter stages of gestation, does usually will seek out specific areas to give birth and raise their fawns. If the habitat does not change noticeably, dominant does will return to the same general area year after year to carry out the fawning process.

Just before giving birth, does will attempt to drive off their buck fawn(s) from the previous year. I've witnessed and photographed this behavior many times. It's not a pretty sight, and it

really can tug at your heart. Although it seems cruel, it is nature's way of insuring that inbreeding does not take place.

## Fawning Time

By late May, the doe's 200-day gestation process is complete and fawning time arrives in the North. If the herd is healthy, most does will give birth to two fawns. Statistically, one is usually a buck and one a doe, with each being similar in size to a loaf of bread and weighing between 6 and 9 pounds. It's been my experience that twins generally are born about 15 to 30 minutes apart. Birth usually is the only time in a fawn's life that it is allowed to nurse while its mother is bedded. It is critical that the fawn gets its mother's first milk as soon as possible. A doe's milk is called colostrum and is loaded with antibodies that boost the fawn's immune system. In addition, a doe's milk is very nutritious and high in energy and fat. By way of comparison, a whitetail's milk is approximately 10 percent fat

*A doe will groom and feed her newborn fawns two to three times a day. During each feeding, a fawn will consume about 8 ounces of milk, which is about 10 percent fat and highly nutritious.*

*At birth, a fawn will often get a lot of attention. This yearling buck cautiously approaches a newborn fawn he found in a clover field. If the doe were to spot this encounter, it would quickly run the buck off.*

while a dairy cow's milk contains roughly 2 to 4 percent fat.

Within minutes of birth, most fawns will attempt to stand and take their first steps. They are very vulnerable to predators at this point, and their survival depends on the doe. Many factors determine whether they will make it through the first week of life.

After giving birth, the doe eats the afterbirth, cleans the area, and bathes her fawns to eliminate scent. This reduces the likelihood of predators locating the newborns. Usually a fawn can walk a short distance within a half-hour of birth. To stay one step ahead of predators, a doe will move her fawns shortly after birth and constantly relocate them during the first few weeks. To enhance survival, a doe will also force her fawns to bed apart and will almost never bed with them.

Generally, a doe will feed and groom her fawns separately, two to three times each day. When a doe seeks her fawn at feeding time, she approaches the fawn's bedding area, uttering mews and low grunts. Once the fawn hears its mother's call, it will rise from its bed and prance to the doe's side before locking on to her nipples and drinking up to 8 ounces of nourishing milk.

Does tend to rule the woods when fawns are vulnerable. Seldom will a doe let another deer get close to her fawns during their first month of life. Over the years I've seen numerous examples of does chasing off curious bucks during this period.

By the time the summer solstice arrives on June 21, most fawns are large and strong enough to outrun the majority of their enemies. Around this time, fawns begin bedding and traveling with the doe wherever she goes. In addition to nursing, fawns will be foraging by the end of June.

# CHAPTER 3

# Slumber Time – Summer

The beginning and end of summer doesn't always coincide with the calendar in my part of the world. I've always thought of summer as the period between Memorial Day and Labor Day. Frost is a real possibility on either side of this time frame, and I find it difficult to associate summer with freezing temperatures.

Two aspects of the whitetail's life—fawning and velvet peeling—also have helped me define the arrival and departure of summer. To me, the seasonal period between each of these events is what summer is all about.

# Food

Whitetails in different regions prefer different natural foods, but regardless of location, about half of their diet should come from natural sources. By the time June arrives, whitetails are flooded with a variety of lush, nutritious forages. During the first part of summer, most foods are in their seasonal prime, offering whitetails an incredible buffet from which to eat. If a whitetail lives in a prime agricultural region, farm crops like clover and alfalfa will provide protein levels exceeding 20 percent.

From a nutritional standpoint, most natural foods don't contain a significant amount of protein. In fact, they seldom have more than 4 to 9 percent protein. However, balance is more important to the whitetail's diet than overall protein content. In total, more than 500 natural foods can comprise a whitetail's diet. These foods can be broken down into six categories: forbs or weeds, grasses, mast, mushrooms, lichens and browse (twigs and leaves). During June and early July, the mixture of agricultural and natural foods is as good as it will be all year, providing ample nourishment for growing fawns and antlers.

Deer are capable of consuming incredible amounts of food during the summer months. Bucks, with their need to support both body mass and antler growth, and lactating does, with their need to feed fawns while maintaining their own bodies, use both natural and agricultural food sources heavily. In studies conducted at my research facility, I've found that mature whitetails will consume up to 15 pounds of lush, green forage a day during late spring and early summer

if the food is available. With the exception of the rut, which occurs during autumn, whitetails are almost always looking for something to eat if they aren't bedded. There's a reason for this.

A deer's rumen (first stomach compartment) is much smaller than that of moose or dairy cattle and cannot digest highly fibrous or lignified foods. Consequently, whitetails need foods with lower fiber and lignin content. From May through June, low-fiber foods are abundant.

*During the first 2 months of life, a fawn's social contacts are limited to its siblings and mother.*

However, by the time July and August roll around, the fiber and lignin levels in many plants can easily double as they mature, making them much less preferred by deer. Because of this, whitetails can become nutritionally stressed in late summer when many of their preferred food sources begin drying up.

## Physical Condition

By the time summer arrives, most whitetails have recovered from any stresses they experienced during the winter months. By June, a deer's summer coat is completely grown in. Also, the abundance of nutritious food allows deer to gain weight. Life is good for the whitetail, but this will change.

As July eases into August, a host of stresses begin affecting deer. Two of the biggest factors are heat and insects. High humidity also takes a toll in some areas. When heat and high humidity arrive, a whitetail's life becomes miserable. The high temperatures often are accompanied by an unbearable onslaught of insects.

***The stress of insects and heat:*** I've photographed whitetails for over 30 years, and I've found the stress that heat and insects place on deer during the summer months can rival the stress of the coldest winter.

During periods of excessive heat and humidity, I've counted up to 100 flies on a deer's body at any one time. This causes whitetails to be in a state of perpetual motion, as they constantly twitch and shake their heads to rid themselves of pests. Such activity will wear down deer, and the bites incurred often cause minor bleeding and even infection.

To escape the flies and other insects, deer will retreat to streambeds or the lowest point in a forest, where air temperatures can be as much as 15 to 20 degrees cooler than in open sun-drenched areas. I've photographed whitetails lying on the cool rocks of a streambed and standing chest deep in water as they attempted to escape insects. Such sights are never pretty, but they always leave me in awe of a whitetail's ability to survive.

I've also seen a situation where a buck's antler velvet was cut and egg-laying flies were attracted to the wound. As a result, maggots formed on the bloody antler, causing the deer to die. Though rare, this is another example of the different types of stress whitetails can face during the "dog days" of summer. Only when late August arrives with its cooler days and nights do whitetails get some relief.

*With testosterone levels at low ebb, bucks become quite social and tolerant of the bucks in their bachelor group. A byproduct of this tolerance is grooming behavior.*

*Mature bucks are quite secretive during the summer months. About the only time they are observed is during the hour on each end of the day.*

The stress that heat and insects can place on whitetails is further compounded when their habitat is poor. Without proper nutrition, the stresses of summer can lead to a host of additional problems for deer, with one of the greatest being disease.

## Home Range

There are three factors that determine the size of a whitetail's summer range—water, food and cover. If each is available, the range of a buck often will be less than 1000 acres. And if food, water and cover are available in above-average quantities, it's not uncommon for a buck's summer home range to be less than 500 acres. This is especially the case in prime farm country.

A doe covers even less ground than a buck while raising her fawns. The New York State Department of Environmental Conservation has an ongoing telemetry study in my area, and the biologists have seen situations where a lactating doe remains in an area smaller than 100 acres for days on end during the summer.

Only under rare circumstances will a doe relocate her fawns during the summer months. Such a move might be caused by a lack of food and water brought on by drought, a forest fire or human intrusion into her territory.

*Few animals are as graceful as a whitetail. Bucks have no problem jumping fences like this three-strand livestock fence.*

## Buck Behavior

Bucks are more secretive during the summer months than at any other time of the year, choosing to bed during the day and feed at night. I have found that it is not uncommon for bucks to remain bedded for more than 90 percent of the daylight hours during the summer. Warm temperatures, insects and the vulnerability of their rapidly growing antlers are the major contributors to this tendency.

With testosterone levels low, bucks become quite social and tolerant of the other members of their bachelor groups. A byproduct of this tolerance is grooming behavior. Prior to the peeling of velvet, it's not uncommon to see mature bucks groom each other as they mingle in feeding areas.

Two types of bachelor groups often exist within a buck population. The first is made up of 1½-year-old "yearling" bucks that have dispersed from their mothers. The second is composed of mature bucks that tend to be more secretive than yearlings.

As in the spring, bucks seldom mingle with does during the summer. About the only time you'll see them close to each other is when they use a common food source.

*Hierarchy:* The process of determining the pecking order within a bachelor group during the summer months is similar to but more intense than the springtime displays of dominance. Behaviors such as the eardrop, the hard look, the snort-wheeze vocalization, and kickboxing are exhibited with greater frequency. This is especially true once bucks' antlers have hardened and the velvet peeling process has been completed.

On several occasions I've watched velvet-antlered bucks hook each other during late August, when the antlers have hardened but not yet peeled. On two occasions in my career I've witnessed velvet-clad bucks actually spar with each other at the end of August. In each case, the bucks came away from the event with bloody strands of velvet hanging from their antler beams. As you'll see in Chapter 4, vicious fights can occur but are quite uncommon.

*When the heat of summer arrives, stress begins to mount on whitetails, especially if the insect count is high. On the day I took this photo in July, the temperature was in the mid-90s. The only way this buck could keep cool and avoid the insects was to stand in the stream.*

Though the hierarchy within a deer herd is far from complete by summer's end, much of the relationship between the old bucks and the younger bucks within a bachelor group has already been determined when September arrives. In most cases the older bucks (3½ to 5½ years old) will dominate the younger animals, making the latter very submissive. Of course, once November arrives and bucks expand their ranges, fights become quite common when they encounter other males not belonging to their core group.

**Signposting:** From late May to mid-July antlers are very fragile. Bucks are more cautious and sedentary in order to minimize antler damage during this time. Consequently, signposting is minimal in May, June and early July. During the latter part of July, however, signposting begins to increase because antler growth is nearly complete.

The majority of signposting during the summer months involves bucks working overhanging licking branches, with mature bucks responsible for most of the activity. When marking these branches, which are usually about 5½ feet off the ground, a buck will salivate on the branch tips and rub his preorbital and forehead glands on the them as well. This method of communication allows a buck to identify himself to every deer living in his area.

Though less common, bucks will sometimes paw or scrape the ground and urinate under the overhanging licking branch during late August or early September. The odor left by the buck's urine in the freshly made scrape is just another way for him to display his presence.

Bucks lightly rubbing their velvet clad antlers on new-growth brush is another signposting behavior I've observed during August, when the antler growing process is complete but the velvet peeling has yet to commence. Scientists have long known that velvet antlers have sebaceous glands, which produce an oily substance called sebum. So, when bucks rub their velvet antlers on brush, they leave a strong scent behind.

## Antler Growth

A buck's antlers grow rapidly with June's long daily photo-period. In most cases, all of the points on a buck's rack will be visible by July 4-10. After this, the points and beams will continue to add length and mass. By the first week in August, the days get noticeably shorter and the antlers stop growing. Toward the end of the month, most antlers are mineralized and hardened and the stage is set for the shedding of the velvet.

*Bucks will work a scrape's overhanging licking branch throughout the year.*

## Doe Behavior

When summer arrives, there is a tremendous amount of activity in a doe's world. In order to properly raise her fawns, a doe must provide the nourishing milk they need to grow and also see to it that they have adequate cover to elude detection by predators.

During the fawn's first 2 months of life, its social contacts are limited to its siblings and mother. As the summer progresses, fawns begin to interact with their older sisters, who are often included in their mother's social group.

Researchers at Cornell University have categorized the suckling stage of a whitetail fawn's life into three phases: seclusion, transition and juvenile ruminant. The seclusion phase generally lasts from birth to about 10 days of age. As the name implies, fawns spend most of this time bedded, relying on their inactivity and speckled coat to keep them out of harm's way. They will generally crouch or hide rather than run when predators pass nearby. During this phase, sibling fawns will bed separately.

The transition phase in a fawn's life generally runs from day 10 to day 50. Rapid growth and change are evident in the fawn's life during this stage. Fawns weigh about 10-12 pounds at the beginning of the transition phase and increase to as much as 35 pounds at the end. During this time, they quickly gain the strength necessary to run from predators. For example, a 10-day-old fawn will be able to outrun most humans; five days later, most natural predators will have a difficult time catching it.

When fawns are 2 to 3 weeks old, they start eating natural vegetation, and by 6 weeks of age their forage intake is usually quite substantial. During this phase of development, siblings will also begin bedding together and spending more time with their mother. Fawns will accompany does in feeding areas like clover and alfalfa fields by the time they reach 6 to 8 weeks of age. At 8 weeks, most fawns weigh 30 to 35 pounds and are ready to progress to the next phase.

Days 50 through 100 generally are considered the juvenile ruminant phase. Many biologists feel that fawns in this stage of development are capable of surviving on their own if their mother is killed. Fawns will continue to actively nurse during this phase, but grazing and foraging will become a more important part of their daily routine. The average body weight of a fawn at this stage of life ranges from 35 to 50 pounds.

For those fawns born in late May and early June, this phase will be nearly complete by the end of August. Once September arrives, a fawn's daily activity routine is very similar to that of an adult deer. They comingle with other deer in feeding areas and, in most cases, lose their spots by mid-September.

*Even after fawns are weaned at about 8 weeks of age, the doe continues to allow them to nurse.*

# CHAPTER 4

# Dawn to Remember

Since the inception of the camera, nature photographers have pursued the whitetail more than any other big-game animal. As a result, virtually every aspect of deer behavior has been captured on film at some point. After photographing and studying whitetails for over 30 years, I thought I had seen it all—until August 30, 2002.

The day began clear and quite cool for the end of August in western New York. The temperature hovered in the low 40s and a spectacular sunrise filled the eastern sky as I headed out for another photo shoot.

I had gone to a nearby clover field several mornings in a row and decided to try the same spot again, hoping to get some pictures of a whitetail buck peeling its velvet. Although I didn't quite get what I was looking for on this morning, I ended up photographing one of the most amazing whitetail encounters ever caught on film.

# The Encounter

Shortly after sunup, I began photographing several deer as they fed before bedding for the day. About 15 minutes into the shoot, two bucks in the field became alert and stared into a nearby apple orchard. Looking to see what had startled them, I noticed a big buck step into the field. He was a mature 11-pointer, and to my delight I could see that he had a couple strands of velvet hanging from his antlers. Immediately I thought, *This is the day I get to photograph a velvet peeling buck.*

Slowly, the big buck began feeding in my direction. After about 10 minutes, he was close enough for me to take a few images with my long telephoto lens. As I looked at him through the camera's viewfinder, I remember thinking to myself, *Come on, pick up your head so I can get a portrait of you.* As soon as that thought crossed my mind, my lens went black as something stepped between the big buck and me. I raised my head from the viewfinder and peered over the camera to see what it was.

*Shortly after the buck that is peeling velvet enters the field to feed, the big 10-pointer approaches.*

A big 10-point buck had blocked my view as he approached the other deer. I had been so focused on photographing the 11-pointer that I failed to notice what else was close by. Slowly, the 10-pointer began circling the velvet-peeling buck. The 10-pointer's gait told me that something wasn't right between the two deer. It didn't take long for the 11-pointer to become irritated. With velvet strands swinging back and forth, he jerked up his head, pulled back his ears, and stepped toward the big 10-pointer in a stiff-legged manner. Based on the body language exhibited by the bucks, it seemed like November.

The 10-pointer didn't appear to be as aggressive. He kept sniffing, checking the wind as if he was trying to smell the blood-soaked velvet that was hanging from the other buck's antlers. It was obvious from the 11-pointer's posture that he didn't appreciate being approached this way.

I couldn't believe what I was witnessing. I was certain something was about to happen, so I checked my viewfinder to make sure I had plenty of film. I was shooting the camera on shutter priority, so I also checked to make sure I had a fast enough shutter speed to catch any action that might materialize. I was good on both points and ready for what I thought would be a typical late-summer encounter between two bucks standing on their hind legs, engaged in a whitetail boxing match. What actually unfolded in the next few moments was far more spectacular.

In the blink of an eye, the bucks came together with all the force of a November brawl. Just before the impact, I started taking pictures. For the next few seconds, my camera's motor drive hummed as the bucks tried to kill each

*Without warning, the two bucks come together with all the force and energy of a November brawl.*

other. I concentrated on keeping the camera focused on the bucks' bodies as they spun around in the dew-drenched clover field. This wasn't easy, but I managed to pull it off. What seemed strange was the absence of the bone-on-bone sound that normally fills the air when two large bucks engage in a fight-to-the-death type of battle. Because both were still in velvet, the skin covering the antlers deadened any noise created by bone-to-bone contact.

The fight was incredible. One second the bucks would be locked up, then each would be trying to get the leverage needed to throw the other to the ground. For a while, I wasn't sure who had the upper hand. Finally, the 11-pointer with the velvet hanging gained an advantage.

*For several seconds, the bucks lock up and push each other around in the dew-covered clover field.*

The 10-pointer realized he was in trouble and tried to retreat. When he turned to flee, his adversary rammed him in the side. The 10-pointer recoiled from the impact and tried to accelerate his getaway, but before he could get any traction, the 11-pointer struck again, ramming him in the hindquarters. After this, the 10-pointer seemed to shift his body into high gear and bolted toward the orchard with the 11-point buck on his tail. The sound of breaking branches resonated across the clover field as the bucks vanished into the orchard. What a rush! The fight ended as quickly as it began.

*Midway into the fight, the velvet-peeling buck gets the upper hand and pushes the 10-pointer sideways.*

## What Happened?

For the next 5 minutes I stayed motionless behind the camera, trying to come to grips with what I had just witnessed. This was truly a first, and I knew that no one would ever believe my story if the pictures didn't turn out. After a 10-day wait, the slides came back, looking just as I hoped they would. When other whitetail enthusiasts saw the photos, they couldn't believe what I had captured on film. To my knowledge, no one has ever photographed such a powerful confrontation between two bucks in velvet.

In retrospect, a couple of factors probably caused these bucks to duke it out on a cool August morning. First, they were undoubtedly vying for territorial dominance, and the 10-pointer simply pushed the 11-pointer's hot button.

Second, just before they engaged, the 10-point buck appeared to be trying to smell the blood on the 11-pointer's peeling velvet. After reliving the moment and studying the slides, I believe the 10-pointer simply was curious about the smell of blood (at least at first) and tried to get a closer look. The 11-pointer didn't appreciate this and decided it was time to show him who was boss.

Regardless of its cause, this was an unbelievably intense fight, and it took place at the least expected time of the year. Watching two bucks do battle while still in velvet is something I'll never forget, and it's one more example of the fact that the more I'm around whitetails, the more I realize how little I really know about them.

The velvet-peeling buck tries to impale the
10-pointer by running his blood-dripping antlers
into the side of the retreating buck.

After regaining his balance, the 10-pointer tries to flee,
but not before being rammed in the rear by the other buck.

# CHAPTER 5

# Peeling the Bone

By the end of August, the stage is set for northern whitetail bucks to begin peeling the velvet from their antlers. This peeling is actually the final chapter in a process that begins in March. As touched upon in Chapter 3, the growth rate of the live antler bone begins to decline as the end of July approaches and the days get shorter. In early August, the growth process ends. This is only an approximate timeline because every buck is slightly different.

As a result of raising whitetails, I've learned that some bucks finish growing their antlers by the end of July, while others continue the growing process until mid-August. On average, though, most bucks complete their antler growth by the first week in August.

Although the hardening process appears to occur suddenly, it is actually quite gradual. The antler's outer layer, which lies just under the velvet skin coating, hardens rather fast during the few weeks before the velvet peels. However, the inner core of the antler takes longer to mineralize and harden. As might be expected, bone formation starts in the lower portion of the antler first and works its way to the ends of the antler beams and points. It's only when the tips of the points harden that the peeling process is set to take place.

*The odor from blood and the commotion velvet-peeling creates attracts other bucks to the peeling event.*

Blood flow to the antler gradually becomes restricted as summer progresses. When the blood flow finally shuts off, the velvet dies. Scientists believe the peeling of the velvet signals the death of the antler bone.

Dermatologists know that human skin begins dying within 6 to 8 hours after blood flow ceases. In addition, significant edema and separation of the skin begins to take place within 48 hours of blood flow ceasing. Because of this, it might be presumed that the actual stoppage of blood flow and the degradation of the velvet is what cause bucks to begin the peeling process.

As antlers harden, they actually shrink. This is most apparent when photographing a whitetail buck over the course of the summer. Around

July 20, the average mature buck's antlers will be maximum size. By mid-August, the same buck's antlers will be noticeably smaller. Throughout the autumn months, a buck's antlers will continue to shrink and become more brittle. Because of this, it is common to see bucks break antler tips during the month before they cast their antlers.

## Who Peels First?

Normally mature bucks peel their velvet first. In all my years of raising whitetails, the peeling process was complete by September 10 for bucks 3½ years of age and older, with the earliest peeling

*During the peeling process, bucks exert an incredible amount of energy as they attempt to rid their antlers of the bloody, smelly velvet. This buck is licking the velvet-peeling blood from his back.*

*Most mature Northern bucks peel their velvet in a 3-week period, from the end of August to mid-September.*

taking place August 28. Yearling and 2½-year-old bucks, on the other hand, have tended to peel their velvet a little later. But regardless of age, I've seldom seen normal, healthy bucks wearing their velvet after September 20 in our area of New York State. On the other hand, I've heard of captive bucks in the South not peeling their velvet until late September or early October.

An interesting side note to the peeling process is that I've been able to track known bucks over the last 15 years, and in nearly every case, once an animal reached 4½ years of age, it would peel its velvet on almost the same day each year thereafter. I've also been able to document that a mature buck will drop his antlers within a day or two of the previous year if he is healthy. This phenomenon is probably a part of each buck's genetic code.

## Fast or Slow?

During the peeling process, a buck expends a tremendous amount of energy attempting to rid the velvet from his antlers. I've photographed many buck fights over the years and few appeared to burn as much energy as the velvet-peeling process does. If a mature buck peels his velvet within 2 hours, he will be physically exhausted by the time he is finished. The panting stupor bucks appear to be in after peeling their velvet is an incredible thing to witness. To illustrate, I'll share an encounter that is typical of the peelings I've seen over the years.

*If the temperature is cool and thick brush is nearby, a buck can complete the peeling process in an hour or less.*

*Few things put more stress on a buck in a short period of time than velvet peeling. If the peeling process is continuous and lasts less than 2 hours, the buck is exhausted when done.*

**Fast action:** On August 31, 1989, while photographing on a large property in eastern New York, I located a mature buck in a swampy area. At first sight I could see that a small piece of velvet had already started peeling from one of his antler tines. From the time I started photographing, it took the buck roughly 50 minutes to completely remove the velvet from his rack.

During the 50-minute period, I was amazed at the buck's behavior as he attempted to strip his antlers clean. Throughout the process, he periodically licked all the blood off the alder brush he was rubbing before peeling more of the velvet. As more of the velvet began hanging from his rack, the buck became increasingly violent in his attempts to remove it. Several times he stopped and panted, exhausted from the ordeal. On two occasions, he actually took a moment to rest before continuing. After all of the velvet had been freed from his antlers, the buck smelled the ground to locate the pieces that had been peeled off. Then, to my surprise, he picked up the strips of velvet and ate them.

In the years since, I've seen this behavior repeated many times. It's believed that bucks

*Velvet-peeling does not cause bucks to bleed to death, it only appears they are in danger of doing so. If the volume of blood under the velvet layer is significant, the peeling process can be messy for a buck.*

commonly eat their velvet for its protein content and to prevent predators from locating them. Whether or not this is true, it's an interesting thing to witness.

Two things that stick in my mind from the 1989 encounter and the several peeling sessions I've witnessed since are the speed at which some bucks remove their velvet and the fury involved in the shedding process.

I have no way of knowing this for sure, but it appears that most bucks hate the smell of blood.

They also seem to be quite irritated by the sight and feel of wet, velvet-covered skin hanging over their eyes and face. It's been my experience that both of these irritants help speed up the peeling process.

**Slow action:** Not all bucks strip and peel their velvet in one frantic event, though. Some may take 2 or 3 days to complete the process. There are even situations where all the velvet does not get shed. I harvested a huge Saskatchewan buck on December 1, 1990, that still had a strip of velvet attached to the back of his antler. However, finding velvet on a buck's rack at this point is certainly an exception to the rule.

Whenever I've had the opportunity to witness bucks peeling their velvet over a span of 2 or 3 days, they appear to complete the process in stages. Once I witnessed a buck peel the velvet off of just two long tines, walk around with the rest of the rack in velvet for a couple days, and then proceed to peel the remaining tines.

*Signposting:* As might be expected, bucks leave an incredible amount of scent in the area where the peeling takes place. In addition to the blood, velvet and glandular odors left behind, a buck will often deposit scent by rubbing and licking the trees and shrubs with his nose and tongue.

People often believe that trees are needed for a buck to peel velvet. This is not the case. In fact, there are many places in North America where there are few or no trees for bucks to rub. In such areas, sage and other brush species work just fine. Even in the Northeast where I live, I've found that bucks prefer to rub off their velvet on shrubs and saplings rather than large trees.

## Transition Step

For all practical purposes, the velvet peeling process and the growth of the winter coat signal the end of the whitetail's summer. Velvet shedding is one of the defining moments in a buck's yearly journey. For me, it marks a seasonal shift and sets the stage for what I view as the whitetail's grandest season—autumn.

# CHAPTER 6

# Apple-Picking Buck

Give a kid a candy bar and he'll want another. Offer an apple to a whitetail and it'll want a dozen more. Like most kids, whitetails have a sweet tooth. Because of this, late summer often finds them gravitating to apple orchards.

There are few foods that whitetails prefer more than apples, and I've often seen deer leave more nutritional food sources in order to satisfy their apple addiction. Knowing this has caused me to focus many of my late-August and early-September photo shoots on apple orchards and the areas surrounding them. Needless to say, the behavior I've been able to record on film has been fascinating and downright humorous at times.

During late summer, nature both teases and frustrates whitetails due to the fact that apples have yet to fall to the ground. With sweet aromas wafting throughout their world, deer often resort to a somewhat unorthodox feeding style in their quest for apples. The accompanying sequence from a recent September illustrates what a whitetail will go through in order to get its apple fix.

*In one motion, the big buck begins to stand in an attempt to reach a low-hanging apple.*

## It's Apple Pickin' Time!

Shortly after daylight, I observed this buck poking through an apple orchard. Based on the way he smelled the ground as he walked, I knew he was searching for apple drops. With few to be found, the buck began looking at and smelling the apples hanging from nearby tree branches.

After checking out several trees, he stopped and looked intently at the apples hanging on a branch just out of his reach.

I could tell from his body language that he was about to stand and attempt to pick the lowest-hanging apple from the tree. In one motion, he pushed off the ground and stood upright. It only took a couple seconds for the buck to steady himself. Slowly he began to take very short steps in the direction of the lowest apple.

*Totally stretched out, the buck tries to decide which apple to pick. He spies an apple a few feet in front of him and begins taking short steps to reach the apple.*

After returning to the ground, he ate quietly while he surveyed more apples hanging overhead. I'm sure he was thinking, *This is easy. As soon as I get this one eaten, I'll go after another.* That's exactly what he did.

It took him about 30 seconds to chew and swallow the first apple before thrusting himself back into the air for another. He got lucky as he picked the second apple because the tree shook, causing several apples to fall from the tree and land on the ground. For the next half-hour the buck vacuumed the ground until all the drops were gone. Then, with the temperature rising and his apple craving satisfied, the buck drifted off into the thick cover of golden rod to bed for the day.

*While taking very small steps, the buck appears to be losing his balance. I thought he was going to return to all fours, but he regained his balance and continued to walk on toward the apple.*

A few seconds into his short walk the buck appeared to momentarily lose his balance. I thought he was going to return to all fours, but he didn't. Instead, he regained his balance, eased to the apple, put it into his mouth, and then returned to the ground. Though it seemed like he was standing for a long time, the buck was probably upright for only 15 to 20 seconds, just long enough to get the job done.

*Got it! With apple in mouth, the buck prepares to return to earth.*

*Once back on all fours, the buck chews and swallows the apple while at the same time looking for the next apple prospect.*

## Unique Behavior?

With the coast clear, I decided to see how high off the ground the apples were hanging. As near as I could tell, they were at least 7 feet high. It's not uncommon for a whitetail to walk upright for a very short distance as it attempts to get its mouth on an apple. However, I'm of the opinion that not all whitetails are pickers. Some deer don't seem to have the ability or the desire to stand and walk for their apples. I base this on the fact that I've observed and photographed many deer that were quite content to let others stand, snap branches and knock the apples off for them rather than doing it themselves. More often than not, I've witnessed both bucks and does simply move on if they couldn't find apples on the ground, even when the overhanging branches appeared to be less than 2 feet from the tips of their noses.

*Once the previous apple is swallowed, the buck immediately rises, attempting to pick another low-hanging apple from the tree.*

# CHAPTER 7

# Transition Time – Early Autumn

Few things in life are as exhilarating as a string of frosty autumn mornings. Add in the chance to witness a forest's green canopy changing to fiery gold and red, and you have the recipe that makes autumn so stimulating to the senses.

Springtime can be truly breathtaking, with birth and rebirth occurring in every corner of the natural world. But autumn has a way of defining life. It uniquely teaches us about the aging process, what has been accomplished, and yes, what lies ahead in the winter.

In many ways autumn is the crowning moment in the whitetail's yearly journey. As September works its way into October, the days are cooler, the air seems fresher, and bucks and does can be found gorging themselves on an abundant array of both hard and soft foods. Each sunset moves the whitetail population one day closer to the annual breeding period. With hormones set to explode, whitetails poise themselves for the fury of the rut.

# Food

By the time the autumnal equinox arrives, both bucks and does are rapidly gaining weight. Research shows it's not uncommon for a buck to increase his body weight by 25 percent from late August to the end of October. This weight gain is the result of the wide variety of highly nutritious foods that are available in most areas at this time of the year. Scientists also believe that deer possess an innate ability to know they must eat to boost fat reserves for the stresses that winter and the upcoming rut will place on them. At any rate, deer are more than willing to take advantage of nature's surpluses during the early stages of autumn.

If available, whitetails gravitate to protein rich foods during spring and summer in order to accommodate their need to supply growing fawns and antlers with required nutrients. Preferred foods vary by region. Once September arrives, their nutritional needs change, and the deer in my area of western New York can be found shifting to carbohydrate-rich foods like acorns, beechnuts, corn and browse. Such foods pack on the fat and supply whitetails with the energy they need. In addition, deer have an insatiable sweet tooth. Consequently, they gravitate to apple orchards and other sources of ripened fruit.

During the autumn months, it is critical that whitetails gain the body mass required to make it through the winter. Because of this, it's not uncommon for bucks and does to consume over 12 pounds of food per day.

*Whitetails have a real sweet tooth. When apples ripen, deer gorge themselves until the available fruit is gone. It's not uncommon for them to consume over 10 pounds of food per day during this time.*

*As autumn inches through October, sparring and fighting become more intense as bucks compete for dominance.*

When the leaves turn golden, whitetails have a tendency to bed for most of the daylight hours, feeding most frequently during the last 2 hours of the day.

Environmental conditions can also dictate when feeding occurs. Baro-metric pressure fluctuations have been known to impact deer feeding tendencies. Several studies have revealed the effects a rising and falling barometer can have on whitetail activity. One such study, conducted by Illinois biologist Keith Thomas, found that whitetails were most likely to feed when the barometric pressure was between 29.80 and 30.29 inches. When the barometer is falling or rising through this range, deer activity should be the greatest.

## Physical Condition

For a whitetail, life during the early autumn is pretty much as good as it gets. Stress is at a low point by the end of September, and the abundance of food and the growth of the winter coat give deer a majestic look at this time of the year.

Unseasonably warm weather is one of the only environmental factors that can cause discomfort at this point. Biologists and hunters have long known that high temperatures can shut down deer activity in a heartbeat. Of all activity suppressors, air temperature is perhaps the most powerful influence on daytime deer movement. During this time of the year, it's not uncommon to have warm days and very cool nights.

Throughout September and the first half of October, deer spend a great deal of time bedded. Warm daytime temperatures have much to do with this. I've observed that it's not uncommon for both bucks and does to remain in one bed for

*Shorter day length and frosty mornings bring on a myriad of changes in whitetail country. One of the most spectacular is the color change.*

up to 4 hours before rising to relieve themselves or move around. Even when they do get up, they may move only a few yards before bedding again.

For the last 8 years, I've been monitoring deer activity with the aid of infrared timers. These devices, known as Trail Timers, record the date and time whenever a deer crosses an infrared beam. What I've discovered in my area of western New York State is quite interesting. When air temperatures rise above 50-55 degrees during September and October, deer activity is significantly curtailed. During the month of November, activity decreases proportionately as the temperature climbs above 45 degrees. Consequently, it's no surprise that deer sightings are relatively low in early autumn. I refer to this as the "fur factor." With a heavy fur coat, a whitetail cannot tolerate heat and is forced to keep its daytime activity to a minimum.

*By mid-October, the bachelor groups that were formed in spring and summer will break up.*

# Home Range

Shortening day length, cooler temperatures and increasing testosterone levels significantly impact the buck population after the 1st of September. Once the velvet-peeling process has been completed, bachelor groups start breaking up as bucks are overcome with an increasing urge to wander.

During late summer, the home range of most bucks is less than 1000 acres. As the calendar inches closer and closer to November, a buck's range expands. By the first of October, it's not uncommon for some bucks to be covering 2000 acres, and by November it's quite typical for a buck to cover over 4000 acres.

For several years, Canadian biologist and hunting guide Louis Gagnon has used trail cameras to monitor buck activity during the autumn months. In one case his cameras photographed a big dominant buck; 36 hours later a hunter he was guiding harvested the same deer 7 air miles away. This is an example of what can be expected when bucks expand their ranges as the rut approaches.

Doe activity during autumn is much more predictable. For the most part, the need to find a new food source is the only thing that will cause a doe to expand her range at this time of the year. Even then, her home range will seldom be more than 1000 acres.

*With each passing day, bucks exhibit more rutting behaviors. Rubbing behavior intensifies as autumn progresses. Rubs are a means for bucks to leave their scent and visual calling card, which alerts other deer to the maker's presence.*

## Buck Behavior

Dominance among white-tailed deer is progressive and ever changing. Once a buck's velvet peels, he begins to ready himself for the upcoming breeding season. In many ways, this period reminds me of an athlete's preseason training regimen. A buck is fat-laden as the summer ends, far different from what he will look like by December 1 when the rut begins to wind down. As the days get cooler through September and October, a multitude of behaviors start to manifest themselves. Throughout forests and fields, rubs and scrapes dot the landscape.

*Rubbing:* Once his antlers are hard, a buck begins to rub more and more frequently as the days shorten. In the process of making rubs, bucks leave visual calling cards. In addition to being dominance markers, rubs are also scent posts. When rubbing his antlers on a tree, a buck will leave scent from his forehead and nasal glands on the rub. In addition, he will almost always lick the surface of the rub to leave his distinct odor. Though other bucks can visually relate the size of the rub to the size of the animal that made it, it is the odor left on the rub by a buck's glands that often lets other deer know who's been there.

**Top:** *October means change to the Northern environment. Temperatures begin falling and heavy precipitation, in the form of cold rain, is not uncommon. This is a harbinger of winter's coming.* **Bottom:** *By the time October bursts onto the scene, bucks will begin paying attention to the does in their territory. Though rare, some Northern does will be bred during October.*

Researchers also believe that the pheromones bucks leave on rubs may serve as a priming function that influences the timing of the rut.

*Scraping:* With ever-increasing levels of testosterone in his system, a buck adds another dimension to his identity by making scrapes. Scraping, like rubbing, allows a buck to make his presence known by dispensing scent throughout his area.

Hunters debate whether scraping is primarily a "buck thing" or if it's done to attract does. In more than 30 years of photographing whitetails from Texas to Canada, I've seen an incredible amount of scraping behavior. In well over 95 percent of my sightings, scraping was done by bucks.

Although does will interact around scrapes, the behavior they exhibit is much different than bucks. A doe will often approach a scrape's licking branch, smell it, and at times even work it the same way a buck will. However, most of the time, a doe will do nothing more than smell it and then move on. After photographing hundreds of bucks making scrapes, my conclusion is that scent marking at scrapes is primarily a buck behavior. It's a way for bucks to leave their "calling card" and show their dominance.

I believe scraping is also a satisfying, conditioned response for bucks. When working an overhanging licking branch, a buck often will appear greatly satisfied by the branch massaging his forehead, preorbital and nasal glands.

I do not believe a buck consciously knows he is spreading his scent to other deer. Judging from the photos I've taken of scraping bucks, it appears the satisfying and stimulating aspects of scraping might largely explain why a buck performs the behavior frequently. I'm not saying scent depositing isn't a big part of scraping, because it is. But I'm convinced the dynamics of scraping are incredibly complex and serve several functions, probably more than we'll ever know.

***Dominance:*** With rubbing and scraping comes physical competition. Once free of velvet, most bucks begin sparring. This is a way to exercise while testing the herd's competitive waters. For the most part, sparring matches are playful skirmishes between two bucks of equal size and stature. However, on occasion, sparring can get out of hand and become ugly during the month and a half that follows the velvet peel.

The best analogy I can offer is that of two teen-age brothers playfully wrestling on the living-room floor. Before they realize it, one gets a bloody nose and tempers flare. While photographing during the fall, I've often seen sparring contests between bucks follow a similar sequence.

By the time late October arrives, the playing is over and most sparring ends until after the rut. At this stage of autumn, a strict dominance hierarchy has been determined and

*By the end of October, scraping behavior is near its peak. When working a scrape's overhanging branch, a buck deposits scent from his nasal, preorbital and forehead gland on the branch. As with rubbing, this behavior telegraphs the buck's presence to other deer in the area.*

*During autumn, does feed heavily and stay within their family group. A doe's home range during autumn is typically 1000 acres or less.*

physical contact between bucks usually will occur only when bucks encounter males they do not know or when a subordinate buck attempts to change the pecking order. Then, true fights can and often do occur. With testosterone at its peak, fights can be incredible and, in many cases, life-threatening to the combatants.

## Doe Behavior

Unlike bucks, which become preoccupied with the rut as autumn progresses, does are content to continue living normally within their family groups. They spend their days bedding and feeding, moving very little. Because of the unpredictable nature of bucks at this time of the year, does make every attempt to avoid them. For the most part, the only time a doe will allow a buck to be near her is when she is in estrus.

If they didn't do so in spring and early summer, most yearling bucks will disperse from their mothers by the time the autumn colors arrive. Sometimes this dispersal takes place on its own, but usually the doe initiates it by harassing the young buck. This is nature's way of preventing inbreeding. Though her fawns are weaned by fall, a doe occasionally will allow them to nurse.

As October winds down, the stage is set for the rut to begin. For the next month, chaos will reign in the whitetail woods as rubbing, scraping, fighting, seeking and chasing becomes the norm. For the whitetail enthusiast, November is a special time.

*By the time autumn's colors peak, bucks will be covering over 2000 acres.*

# CHAPTER 8

# Touched By Light

*"And God said, 'Let there be lights in the expanse of the sky to separate the day from the night, and let them serve as signs to mark seasons and days and years, and let them be lights in the expanse of the sky to give light on the earth.' And it was so. God made two great lights – the greater light to govern the day and the lesser light to govern the night. He also made the stars. God set them in the expanse of the sky to give light on the earth, to govern the day and the night, and to separate light from darkness. And God saw that it was good. And there was evening, and there was morning – the fourth day."* (Genesis 1:14-19, NIV).

After practically living with nature for over half a century, I'm still in awe of the way God pieced our universe together. What a creator! Everything He created is precise and perfect. Each natural phenomenon has a reason for existing. It's truly amazing how the natural world influences every aspect of the whitetail's life.

For the last 8 years, Vermont wildlife biologist Wayne Laroche and I have been researching the influence the moon has on the timing of the whitetail rut in the North, specifically north of the 35th latitude. In its eighth year, the project is expected to run for 15 years before being completed. Why so long, you ask? There are a number of reasons, but the primary factor is the fluctuation in the timing of what we refer to as the whitetail's rutting moon, which is the second full moon after the autumnal equinox.

Those who have followed our work know that the timing of the rutting moon comes within a day or two of repeating itself every 11 years and reasonably close to repeating itself every 3 to 4 years. Consequently, it's important to collect good data over an extended period of time in order to evaluate the moon's impact on white-tailed deer rutting activity.

## Genesis of the Work

Though we've been collecting data for the last 8 years, our interest in this project was born over 15 years ago.

Laroche is a respected fisheries biologist. He is also an avid whitetail hunter who spends the entire month of November in northern Maine chasing big woods bucks. He became interested in the moon's influence on whitetails after researching the impact the moon has on grouper fish in the Caribbean and the Gulf of Mexico. As he hunted the Maine woods every year, he noticed distinct fluctuations in whitetail activity patterns. After studying the yearly changes, he began to wonder if the moon was affecting the way whitetails behaved during November, just as it had influenced the fish he had studied over the years.

My interest in lunar-related behavior began in the mid-1980s while hunting and photographing. Up until then I had bought into the research data that originated in the 1950s and '60s that said the peak breeding period for whitetails in my region of the North (42nd latitude) would be November 15-20 each year.

Over a 10-year period (1985-1995), I had the opportunity to photograph whitetails extensively on a large property in the Adirondack Mountains of New York. During this time, I shot hundreds of rolls of film and kept detailed notes on deer behavior. Despite the deer population and the adult doe-to-antlered buck ratio remaining constant, the peak breeding period was seldom the same from year to year. Some years the breeding took place in early November, some years mid-November, and some years late November. It was obvious to me that something more than photoperiod, or shortening day length, was driving the timing of the rut's seeking, chasing and breeding phases.

*Rubs like this are true buck scent posts. When I photographed this rub, the buck worked the tree for more than 5 minutes. He'd rub for a while, then lick and sniff the bark before continuing to rub.*

*During the week after the rutting moon, a buck begins to pursue every doe in its territory.*

In the early '90s, I became aware of work Laroche was doing that dealt with the relationship between the width of a whitetail's track and its body size. To learn more, I interviewed him for a magazine article I was writing. We shared many things about ourselves and our love for whitetail hunting. During the course of our discussion we talked about the variations we were seeing in the timing of whitetail rutting behavior. I'll never forget Wayne's comment that he believed the moon was responsible for the fluctuations in deer activity that we were observing during November. After our conversation, we decided to see if the moon had anything to do with the timing of the whitetail rut.

## The Hypothesis

As further background, I'll offer the hypothesis for our research. At some point in autumn, the amount of daylight decreases enough to reset the whitetail's reproductive clock, thus placing the breeding season in November, December and January in the Northern Hemisphere. Once the doe's reproductive cycle is reset by a specific amount of daylight, her estrous cycle is ready to be cued by moonlight, which provides a bright light stimulus to the pineal gland several nights in a row each lunar month. Then, the rapid decrease in lunar brightness during the moon's third quarter triggers hormonal production by the pineal gland. Physiological

*Trail Timers are instrumental in our research. Up to 12 are used at any one time and record the month, day, hour and minute a deer passes. The data is downloaded to computers.*

changes prompted by the pineal gland culminate in ovulation and estrous.

A northern doe's estrogen level peaks around November 1, as does a buck's sperm count. With both sexes poised to breed, it stands to reason a mechanism must be in place if the doe is to enter estrous and be bred under the darker phases of the moon, which are the third through the first quarters. That mechanism in the North (north of about the 35th latitude) is usually the second full moon after the autumnal equinox, which we call the rutting moon.

## What We Know at Halftime

With each passing year, we've added more and more data collection devices to the research project. In the beginning, we monitored just six does. Now, we are collecting data for our research from nearly 100 does.

We also monitor air temperature, weather patterns and moonlight intensity throughout the fall. In addition, we have 12 Model 500 Trail Timers to record deer activity throughout each day. Four of the timers are in my farm's 35-acre high-fenced whitetail research facility and, at any one time, up to eight are positioned in other areas of our farm to monitor the wild, free-ranging deer population. The data, which is collected from October through December, is downloaded to our computers for analysis.

Unlike 8 years ago, when no one was helping us, we now have several serious deer hunters and outfitters across North America (who are in the

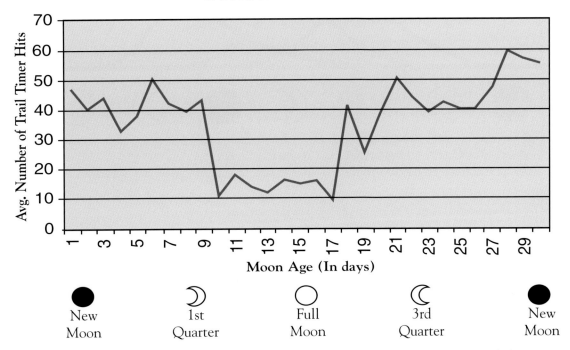

**Figure 1.** *After 8 years and over 15,000 data points, our research has shown (with one exception) deer activity on average to be quite similar throughout the October-to-December study period. The exception is November's rut, which is illustrated in Figure #2. Of note, the one-week period between the first and second quarter has always recorded the least deer activity of all lunar periods.*

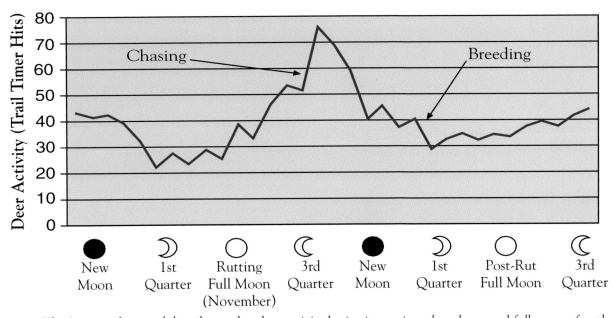

**Figure 2.** *The 8 years of research has shown that deer activity begins increasing when the second full moon after the autumnal equinox arrives and peaks a couple days after the third quarter. Breeding data has shown that the majority of breeding occurs from the third to first quarter that follows the rutting moon.*

*Seeking Phase*  *Chasing Phase*  *Breeding Phase*

| New Moon | 1st Quarter | Rutting Moon Full Moon | 3rd Quarter | New Moon | 1st Quarter | Full Moon |

*This chart illustrates when the rut's seeking, chasing and breeding phases blend into each other in relation to the rutting moon, which is by definition the second full moon after the autumnal equinox.*

woods every day during the fall) keeping detailed journals to chronicle deer behavior in their regions of the country. This added information has allowed us to better understand what is happening in other parts of North America during October, November and December.

With well over 15,000 data points in our system, we've concluded that the second full moon after the autumnal equinox stimulates both buck and doe rutting activity. After 1999 we made a concerted effort to step up our data collection, primarily because of the way the rutting moon was going to occur in 2000, 2001 and 2002. Though the rutting moon was 11 days apart in 2000 and 2001, the rutting behavior was classic—just as predicted. In 2000, the rutting moon was November 11 and in 2001 it fell on November 1.

In all reporting locales but one, the seeking phase of the rut kicked in just as expected in 2000, around the 8th of November; breeding activity took place from November 17 to the end of the month.

In 2001, things were again on target, but earlier than in 2000 since the rutting moon was

*By November, a buck's testosterone will have peaked.*

November 1. The United States experienced one of its warmest autumns on record in 2001, which brought daytime deer activity to a screeching halt in many places. However, when the air temperature was less than 45 degrees during the day, everyone collecting data reported that chasing activity was intense during the first week of November. By November 10, it was obvious that the breeding was full blown, and by November 20, most of the primary breeding was over. So, the data collected in 2000 and 2001 almost perfectly matched the research findings from 1995 and 1998, respectively, when the rutting moon fell on similar dates.

Based on past data, we know that when the rutting moon falls anywhere from late October to November 12, the timing of the seeking, chasing and breeding phases of the rut is very predictable; we refer to this as a "classic rut."

During the years when the rutting moon appears later (like 2002, when it occurred on November 19), we've discovered that the timing of the rut's seeking, chasing and breeding phases is just a little different. When the rutting moon arrives after November 13-14, we've found that the rut progresses more rapidly than when the rutting moon arrives earlier in the month.

Basically, the data are showing that when the rutting moon arrives late, the seeking begins 3 or 4 days before the full moon, just as we've always predicted. However, we've discovered that once the full moon occurs, the chasing is frenzied and the breeding kicks in within a day or 2 of the full moon's appearance rather than a week after its arrival, as it does in years when the rutting moon appears in early November. The 2 years in our research project that illustrate this are 1997, when the rutting moon was November 14, and 2002, when it arrived on November 19.

In 1997, the data showed that the seeking and chasing phases of the rut didn't happen until

*By the time the rutting moon is full, bucks will be in a scraping frenzy. During the week after the rutting moon, it's not uncommon for sexually active bucks to make over 10 scrapes a day.*

November 12-21. Breeding kicked in within a couple days of the rutting moon and ran through the end of the month.

The 2002 findings are nearly identical to 1997. In 2002, all but one reporting location indicated seeking and chasing peaked between November 16 and November 22 in the North. Breeding began around the 19th and 20th and peaked Thanksgiving week (November 24-28). There also was a fair amount of breeding still occurring the first few days of December. Looking to the future, I feel confident that the northern whitetail rut in 2005 and 2013 will be very similar. This prediction is based on the consistency of our data from 1997 and 2002.

*With a buck's range now expanded to 4000 or more acres, fights with other dominant bucks are inevitable. Such encounters are usually incredible and can result in the death to one or both of the bucks.*

## Rut Suppressors

To varying degrees the project has revealed several factors that can affect the amount of deer activity observed during daylight hours.

***Air temperature:*** Temperature readings and the Trail Timer data indicate that when the daytime temperature rises above 45 degrees during November, deer activity comes to an abrupt halt. With their heavy fur coat and inability to ventilate as humans do, deer simply cannot function in warm weather.

***Sex ratio:*** Adult doe-to-antlered buck ratios greater than 3-to-1 also decrease deer activity during the three phases of the rut. This is primarily due to the fact that does are less active than bucks in November. With far more does than bucks in a population, every available buck is with a doe when the hot-to-trot rut arrives. On the other hand, in areas where the adult doe-to-antlered buck ratio is 1-to-1 or 2-to-1, buck activity is greater because there are far fewer does

to go around, resulting in competition between bucks for breedable does. As one might expect, we also see greater buck activity in populations that have more mature bucks in the herd.

***Human pressure:*** The impact of human pressure is perhaps the "mother of all rut suppressors," especially when daytime air temperatures rise above 45 degrees. Going into this project, I had a feeling human presence in

the deer woods would affect movement, but I didn't realize the impact would be so great. The Trail Timer data show that approximately 55 percent of deer movement occurs during daylight hours in areas where there is little or no human presence. In areas where there is moderate to heavy human activity in the form of hikers, birders, or hunters, only about 30 percent of deer movement takes place during daylight.

## The Maine Lab

In order to get a better read on the moon's influence on whitetail rutting behavior, Laroche and I have started to look more closely at how deer move in areas where humans, poor adult doe-to-antlered buck ratios, warm temperatures, and baiting have a minimal impact. There are few places in the United States where such conditions exist, but northern Maine is one of them.

The whitetails found in this region are not pressured by man, nature keeps the adult doe-to-antlered buck ratio at less than three to one, baiting is not allowed, and warm temperatures are not as common as they are in other regions of the country. What makes Maine so unique is that it has mature bucks in the population, and snow is often present to tip off serious trackers as to what is going on in the deer world. So, with few rut suppressors present, the far-northern portion of this vacationland is the ultimate place to study the moon's effect on deer activity.

*By the time all the leaves have fallen from the trees, the stage is set for the arrival of the rutting moon and the onset of the rut.*

*If air temperatures are cooler than normal for an area, buck activity will be high during the seeking and chasing phase of the rut.*

As mentioned earlier, Laroche spends the entire month of November in a northern Maine deer camp, living out of an 18'x52' wall tent. His camp is limited to eight hunters at a time, and each night Laroche debriefs every hunter, asking them to recall the number of scrapes and rubs observed, the number of deer sightings by sex, the types of behavior witnessed, and any other species of animals that were seen. This data is then analyzed and incorporated into our database. Laroche and his party cover a remote area of 50 to 100 square miles on any given day.

Dick Bernier is a hunting legend in the state of Maine. He's written two popular books on tracking white-tailed deer, and like Laroche, he and his father spend the entire month of November in the northern Maine bush tracking the biggest bucks they can find.

Interestingly, Bernier and his father realized long ago that there was a correlation between November's full moon and the timing of the whitetail's rut. When I began writing about the moon's impact on the rut for *Deer and Deer Hunting* magazine, they contacted me to let me know they concurred with the findings of our research. They also offered access to their records. So, at the end of each day, they log everything they observe into their journals and forward this information to Laroche and me. As one might expect, the observations of Laroche's party and the Berniers have nearly mirrored each other.

## Synopsis

Enlightening is one of the best words I know of to describe this research project. It amazes me that the relationship between the moon and the timing of the rut was not discovered long ago. We set out to run the project for 15 years, and although we could probably wrap it up now because of the repeatable patterns we've observed and documented, we fully expect to continue for the remaining 7 years. Simply put, our fascination with the project keeps our interest level high.

In 1999, I wrote *Hunting Whitetails by the Moon*. Chapter 16 of this book, "Predicting the Future," was based on what I knew at the time. Because of what has been learned since then, I now know the predictions that were offered for 2005 and 2013 are a bit off. However, they easily can be adjusted by studying the following paragraphs.

As a quick recap, keep in mind that the seeking, chasing and breeding phases of the northern whitetail rut will occur as follows:

- When the second full moon after the autumnal equinox falls between late October and November 12, the seeking phase of the rut will start approximately 3 to 4 days before the full moon and run 3 to 4 days after it. The chasing phase will kick in a couple of days after the full moon and be intense for about 10 days following the full moon. The breeding phase will begin about 7 days after the full moon and last about 14 days thereafter if the herd is fine-tuned (meaning it has good nutrition, good habitat, a good sex ratio, and a well represented mature buck population). Note that the phases will overlap somewhat.

- When the second full moon after the autumnal equinox occurs November 13 or later, the seeking phase will begin approximately 3 days before the full moon. However, the chasing phase will begin a little earlier than normal, and the breeding phase will occur from the full moon to 14 days thereafter in fine-tuned herds. So, when the rutting moon appears late, the breeding phase takes place a little sooner than when it appears in early November.

Not everyone has the flexibility to block out the whole month of November in order to have a ringside seat for the whitetail rut. The benefit of this research is the ability to let hunters and deer lovers know the optimal times to hunt and observe the whitetail rut.

*When a doe nears estrus, a buck will do everything in his power to ensure he gets the breeding rights.*

# CHAPTER 9

# Seeking Time

I've come to realize that no two ruts are ever alike. Some autumns, the rut starts like a lamb, and other years it crashes onto the scene like a lion. Regardless of its intensity, however, the whitetail's rut can be divided into three phases—seeking, chasing and breeding. The seeking stage is the beginning of the rutting ritual.

By the time the rut's seeking phase arrives, bucks are very adventurous. In order to investigate all the doe groups in their expanded home range, bucks are constantly on the move. Their feeding habits during the three phases of the rut resemble pit stops at fast-food establishments, and their caloric burn far exceeds their food intake. In addition, bucks are more vocal in autumn than at any other time of the year. By November, they communicate with other deer by emitting grunts, bleats, snorts and snort-wheezes on a regular basis.

With testosterone at maximum flow, bucks feverishly search for estrous does when the seeking phase arrives. Their noses dictate when and where they go. No doe group is safe as bucks move across their expansive range. At this time, all the dynamics of buck behavior unite. Bucks are now finely tuned physical specimens that spend every waking hour rubbing, scraping and looking for does. During the last several years, my research has shown that a sexually active buck may make 6 to 12 scrapes per hour during this phase of the rut. However, not all bucks are sexually active, and the frequency of a buck's scraping activity usually depends on his sex drive.

Lip-curling—a behavior scientists call "Flehmening"—is extremely common during the rut's seeking phase, and bucks can be expected to lip-curl wherever a doe has urinated. Many scientists believe that lip-curling allows a buck to learn if a doe is entering estrous. During this process, a buck traps scent from a doe's urine in his nose and mouth. This allows a buck's scent-analyzing device—the vemero-nasal organ in the roof of his mouth—to determine a doe's status.

When a mature buck or an aggressive yearling encounters a stranger or a recognized contender, one or two things usually occur.

Stare-downs or shadowing generally take place first. Most bucks are aware of the size of their own antlers and body, and can quickly size up a situation. A difference in antler size and body size will often cause the inferior buck to cut short the encounter by shying away. However, if two bucks of similar size—with testosterone-injected attitudes to match—cross paths, the results can get ugly in a hurry.

If a fight to the death begins, the scene can be spectacular. Antlers become ice picks, and there are no rules of engagement or fair fighting. A buck's objective is to knock his opponent to

*During the seeking phase of the rut, bucks are loners and cover a considerable amount of territory checking various doe family groups.*

*Bucks often work and rework scrapes located in heavily-used travel corridors. For this reason, they can be very predictable during the seeking phase of the rut.*

the ground, then stick his antlers into the opposition's abdomen or hindquarters. Such fights can be gruesome, and when they are over, both the victor and loser often need time to recover before resuming their pursuit of does. Combatants can even die from their wounds.

From a hunting standpoint, the seeking phase is one of the best times to be in the woods, especially for a tree-stand hunter. As mentioned in the last chapter, the peak of this period is usually 3 to 4 days before and 3 to 4 days after the rutting moon. During this time, bucks are on the move but not yet chasing every doe they encounter. Funnels, scrape lines and rub lines are more predictable to hunt during this period than

at any other time of the rut. Unfortunately, the seeking phase only lasts a short time before blending into the chase phase.

## Doe Behavior

*Oh, no, here comes the storm!* If I were a whitetail doe, this is what I would be thinking when the seeking phase kicks in.

When this stage of the rut is about to burst onto the scene, does are content. They've spent the fall minding their own business, hanging out with their female family members and going about each day in much the same manner as they did during the previous two months. However, when bucks kick off the first stage of the rut, does go on red alert. With males in seek mode, does become more wary and secluded. They move less, knowing that it won't be long before they'll be chased by every buck they encounter.

For the most part, bucks cruise from one doe group to another trying to find an estrous female during the rut's seeking phase. When the seeking phase begins, does will merely move off when a buck approaches. Seldom will bucks pursue them at this point, opting instead to check each doe's bed or the area where does were feeding before moving off to check another group of females. Once the buck has left, does will revert to what they were doing before the buck disrupted them.

## A Day in the Life

Long shadows cast an eerie pattern on the moonlit forest floor. With the moon inching toward the horizon, the big 10-point rose from his bed. He'd been resting for over 3 hours, and with dawn fast approaching, it was time to cover some ground before daybreak. After stretching and urinating in his bed, he stood motionless for a few moments. With the November full moon showing the way, he began walking. Food was no longer on his mind; does were.

Slowly he began covering ground, stopping every so often to smell the air and listen to the sounds of the fading night. The full moon's light made it easy to find his way in the forest. About a quarter mile into his trek, he slowly crossed a stream. Loose stones clattered underfoot as he made his way through the shallow water. In one fluid motion the buck catapulted his 250-pound frame onto the stream bank and headed up a steep incline that led to a clover field. At the

field's edge, he paused. A hundred yards away, several does and fawns were filling their bellies one last time before dawn. All was calm. Each deer in the field was focused on him, perhaps wondering what he was going to do next.

The 10-pointer walked to the edge of the woods and stopped under a stub of an oak branch that hung about 5½ feet off the ground. He reached up to touch it, arching his back to gain more height. Feverishly, the monarch began rubbing his nasal, preorbital and forehead gland on the overhanging branch. The sound of his massive antlers whacking against it could be heard for nearly 100 yards. After working the branch, he pawed the ground beneath it several times before slowly positioning his hind feet under his body so that his tarsal glands touched. Urine began to rain down over the rank tufts of tarsal hair, saturating the ground. The process of working the branch, pawing the earth and urinating had only taken a minute to accomplish, but the odor left behind would be enough to alert every deer in the area that he'd been there. All this time the deer in the field watched intently, waiting for the buck's next move.

With the moon's rays glistening off his antler tines, the buck moved toward the does. They quickly trotted into the thick cover at the edge of the field. Instead of chasing them, the buck walked to where the does had been feeding. At each site, he smelled for urine. In the two locations where the does had urinated, he licked and smelled the ground for a few seconds before raising his head to lip-curl. This was his way of telling if any of the does were in or coming into estrous. None were.

With the scent-checking process complete, he slowly zigzagged his way across the field before

*If an area has a good population of mature bucks, rubbing sign will be heavy during the seeking period.*

entering the woodlot on the other side. The does he had just encountered showed no signs of being in estrus, so it was time to look for another doe group. Within minutes of the buck's departure, the does reentered the clover field and continued to feed.

As soon as the 10-point entered the woods, he went on alert. Something caught his eye in the moonlit forest. Another deer was heading his way. The big buck stood motionless as the inquisitive deer approached. He could tell by its gait that it was an 8-pointer he knew well. They had been around each other often, having spent the summer in the same bachelor group. But things were different now. With the rut heating up quickly, the days of being buddies were over for a while.

When the small 8-point came within 15 yards, the big buck dropped his ears, brought his head up and began to approach the lesser deer. The hair bristled on the massive 10-pointer's neck and back. Without warning, he let out a thunderous grunt-wheeze. In an instant, the small

*Because of the scent left by bucks on rubs, rivals will often stop to smell a rub made by another buck.*

*Does rapidly become wary of approaching bucks during the seeking phase. In most cases, a buck will not chase a doe during this time.*

8-pointer wheeled and ran off through the woods, breaking branches as he went. Soon, the forest was quiet again.

The smell of freshly fallen acorns that permeated the area enticed the buck. After sniffing the ground for a few seconds, he ate several before continuing his journey. The sound of crisp leaves crunching underfoot made it difficult to hear, so he paused every few yards to survey the surroundings. The forest was beginning to wake with the arrival of daylight. In the distance, a crow cawed incessantly while a blue jay scolded from a nearby tree. As the full moon dropped to the horizon, the first shafts of sunlight began hitting the frost-tipped tree branches overhead. The buck spotted movement in front of him. Several does were feeding on the abundant acorn crop. He stood motionless, surveying the situation before moving closer.

Within a few feet of the buck was a baseball bat-sized aspen tree. Slowly he approached the tree and began rubbing his big rack on it. After a couple scours, he sniffed and rubbed his nose on the freshly shredded bark. Every so often the buck would look up to check on the does. They had not wandered away. For the next 5 minutes, he thrashed the tree until half of its bark was removed.

With shreds of aspen bark clinging to his antlers and hanging in his eyes, the big buck picked up movement near the does. A buck was walking in his direction, silhouetted against the rising sun. The big 10-pointer recognized him. It was another mature buck, an 8-pointer he had encountered many times in the past. The dominant 10-pointer approached the big 8-point.

At 10 yards, the 10-point lowered his head, dropped his ears and bristled his fur like a pincushion. The 8-pointer slowly eased around him. He too had dropped his ears and bristled his coat. Each buck rolled his eyes and cocked his head. The rut's fury was about to manifest itself.

With the does standing nearby, the bucks came together with all the energy their big bodies could muster. The combined sound of breaking branches, rustling leaves, clashing antler tines, moans, and grunts was deafening. Something had to give.

*With each passing day, the competition and attitude level of dominant bucks rise. It's not uncommon to witness one dominant buck chasing another similar size buck.*

*Though does steer clear of bucks during the autumn months, they capitalize on every opportunity to feed. If food sources like apples are plentiful, they will consume over 10 pounds of food a day.*

Realizing he was no match for the 10-pointer, the smaller buck struggled to his feet and ran off through the woods with the big 10-point in tow. The victor gave up the chase after 30 yards.

The dominant buck stood panting in the autumn sun. Each breath he exhaled resembled a blast of steam being shot into the air. After a few moments, the woods came alive again. The does had left, but three subordinate bucks that had heard the fight were now milling around less than 50 yards away. The big buck looked in their direction and snort-wheezed. The aggressive vocalization convinced the smaller bucks to disperse.

With their antlers locked, the big 10-point drove the 8-pointer into a small sapling. The 8-point lost his balance and fell to the forest floor, exposing his side to his opponent. In a lightning-quick move, the 10-pointer tried to gore the 8-point in the side. A split second before impact, the 8-pointer thrust his body sideways enabling him to take a glancing blow rather than a direct hit from one of the 10-pointer's long tines. Hair flew from the buck's side as he tried to get out of the way.

After checking for doe sign and eating a few acorns, the 10-point began following the does' trail, which took him to a cedar swamp. By now, the November sun was getting high in the sky. The buck had been on his feet for over 4 hours. On a small hummock in the swamp, he decided to bed.

For the next 5 hours, he dozed and took in all the sounds of the forest. Nearby, red squirrels and chipmunks scurried about. Chickadees fluttered among the low hanging hemlock and cedar branches, looking for seeds.

Around mid-day, the 10-pointer rose from his bed, stretched, and moved off along a game trail through the swamp. Every 50 to 100 yards the buck stopped to work an overhanging licking branch, and at some scrapes he took the time to

*During the seeking phase of the rut, bucks check every doe's bed in hopes of locating one that has come into her estrus period.*

paw the ground and urinate. In several locations, he found beds where does had been lying. At each spot, he checked for urine and the odor of estrous.

When the buck reached the far side of the swamp, he stopped to make a rub on a big cedar tree. The pungent odor of the tree's bark enticed him to rub for 10 minutes, longer than normal. By the time he finished, the burrs at the base of his antlers were plugged with bark. With the temperature above normal, it was time to bed again.

Only an hour of daylight remained when the big buck decided to rise and look for does. He felt the pangs of hunger in his belly, but the urge to procreate was greater than his desire for food.

Heading into a slight breeze, the 10-point cautiously poked his way through the hardwoods toward a standing cornfield. He exited the woods in a corner, where the corn came right up to the forest. Before entering the field, he stopped to work a licking branch and freshen a scrape with his urine.

Only 2 weeks before, the big buck would have come to this cornfield to eat. Now he came looking for does. He listened for the sound of deer feeding on the dried ears of field corn. The breeze rustled the cornstalks just enough that he couldn't tell if there were deer in the area. He walked the field's edge to the adjoining alfalfa plot, pausing at the point where the corn and alfalfa fields came together. Not far away, a doe and two fawns were feeding. Slowly the 10-point walked toward the doe. When she saw him coming, she bolted into the corn with her fawns close behind. The buck's nose took him to where the doe had been standing. He sniffed the area and found urine. A hard lip-curl detected nothing. He fed a little before heading back into the woods as nightfall descended.

For the next 3 hours, the big 10-point cruised from doe group to doe group, stopping only to make a rub, work a scrape, and take a few mouthfuls of food. Several times he encountered other bucks, but in each case they were subordinate to him and unwilling to challenge his dominance. The rutting urge was increasing, and he knew he needed to find an estrous doe. This was what he lived for.

With a full moon overhead, the tired buck bedded along a ridge overlooking a deep ravine. He'd covered a lot of ground and needed some rest before the next day arrived. As he dozed in the shadow of a hemlock tree, he knew the best was yet to come.

*As the seeking phase blends into the chasing phase of the rut, bucks begin to chase every doe they encounter.*

# CHAPTER 10

# Chasing Time

Bucks truly go bonkers during the chasing phase of the rut. Because this period overlaps a portion of the seeking phase, the two stages are often confused. However, they are different in spite of the overlap.

The chasing phase usually begins 2 or 3 days after the rutting moon and lasts 3 or 4 days into the full-blown breeding phase. During the chasing phase, does are close to entering estrus, and bucks are frantically trying to be the first to find them. This is a time when a buck will chase every doe he encounters. Such meetings often resemble a cutting horse trying to cut a calf out of a herd of cows. A buck can be persistent, knowing he will eventually find a doe that won't run. During the chasing phase, scraping and rubbing continue, and in many cases can be intense, especially in a well-tuned herd. The chasing phase often brings more powerful fights, especially if two bucks pursue the same doe.

During the week or so prior to the chasing phase, bucks cover a tremendous amount of ground as they go from doe group to doe group seeking an estrous female. As the previous chapter explained, not much chasing occurs during the seeking phase. However, as the seeking phase blends into the chasing phase, this changes considerably and sleep is nearly non-existent for bucks. No doe is safe from a buck's harassment during this time, as chaos comes to the deer woods when the chasing phase explodes. This is also the time that bucks are very vulnerable to hunters.

## Doe Behavior

For the most part, does' behavior during the chasing phase mirrors that of the pre-rut and the seeking phase. They'll spend their days living with their family groups. However, the attention they get from bucks causes them to be more wary of males. During the chasing phase, bucks lose all sense of civility in their pursuit of does. If there is a time when does fear for their well-being, this is it. Bucks have been known to gore and kill does that try to flee from their advances.

The changes in a doe's body chemistry during this time are very interesting. Progesterone levels drop and estrogen levels rise rapidly beginning 7 days before estrus. Hormone levels change in urine as they change in blood. Bucks, with their highly sensitive olfactory organs, detect these changes through Flehmening, or lip-curling. These changes cause bucks to literally go ballistic. Consequently, a buck's every waking hour turns into perpetual motion during the chasing phase, as the search for does that are in estrus or coming into estrus shifts into high gear.

## A Day in the Life

When we left the big 10-pointer during the seeking phase (Chapter 9), he had bedded down after a day of cruising his territory. Several days have passed, and he's found himself in the middle of the rut's chasing phase.

A mixture of sleet and rain had been falling for most of the night. As the gray dawn arrived,

*When two mature bucks cross paths during the rut, one will usually try to exert his dominance over the other in the form of ear-drop, bristling his fur and shadowing.*

*During the seeking and chasing phase of the rut, fighting is a common behavior. Such fights seldom last longer than 1 or 2 minutes before the lesser buck breaks and runs for cover.*

the precipitation stopped. It was cold in the forest, near freezing. With water still dripping from the tree branches, the big buck rose from his bed. After stretching, he shook his body to rid himself of the water that had accumulated on his back. Without hesitation he began walking into the slight breeze coming from the west. He was anxious to find an estrous doe.

It didn't take him long to exit the woods. In front of him was a sea of golden rod. Twenty yards into the wet fallow field, he picked up the scent of another deer, a doe. Though he couldn't see her, she was emitting a strong odor. Slowly he walked through the head-high weeds, following the lead of his nose. After going 100 yards, the doe jumped up in front of him and ran for the woods. The 10-pointer paused for only a moment before taking up the chase. Within seconds he was at full stride, chewing up 20 to 30 feet of ground with each bound.

By the time he reached the woods' edge, he had caught up with the doe. Thirty yards into the woods, the doe slithered into the center of a big blowdown and stopped. The frustrated buck came to a screeching halt 5 yards away. For the next minute, the two deer stood and looked at each other. All the while, the big buck emitted a continuous flow of medium-volume grunts, known to biologists as tending grunts. Periodically the buck would stomp his front hoof on the ground. Drool was now dripping from the corner of his mouth. He was ready to breed, but the doe wasn't.

The buck made a bluff at the doe, like he was going to try to break into her forest refuge. Though he knew he could not get his antlers through the tight tangle of vines and treetops, the doe thought he could, so she bolted off through the woods. The massive buck tore around the blowdown in hot pursuit. The commotion was

*During the chase phase, bucks lose all sense of civility in their pursuit of does. If there is a time in a doe's life when she fears for her own well being, this is it.*

impressive, and in spite of the damp conditions, branches could be heard breaking for a considerable distance.

After 100 yards, the doe came to a small stream. Rather than jumping across, she turned and ran downstream. The big buck was right on her tail. Water splashed from side to side as they ran. Just as the doe jumped up onto the stream's bank, the buck gave off a loud bellowing grunt that sounded almost like a death moan. He was really frustrated now. The doe immediately found shelter in another blowdown, a big oak treetop containing a tight crevasse that was big enough only for her.

The noise of the chase had attracted other bucks. Competition was forming. With the big

buck standing only 20 yards from the stream's edge, the clatter of rocks coming together in the stream caused him to turn and look in that direction. A yearling buck and a 3½-year-old 8-pointer were crossing the stream. The 10-point wheeled and ran toward them, grunting with each step he took. When he had cut the distance in half, the yearling snorted. The dominant buck was prepared to do anything necessary to get them away from the doe. He charged the 8-point as it was trying to escape, ramming his antlers into the subordinate buck's flank. The impact knocked the 8-point to the ground, but an instant later the smaller buck was back on his feet and running through the woods. The big buck ran after him, but gave up the chase after 75 yards.

With the bucks momentarily out of sight, the doe left the blowdown and headed off through the woods. The big buck decided not to pick up the chase. After standing near the stream's edge for a few minutes, he began following it in a southerly direction, looking for more doe sign.

It had been some time since the buck had left his pre-dawn bed. In spite of being sleep deprived, he remained energized thanks to a healthy dose of adrenaline. Every hundred yards or so, he stopped to work a scrape, and twice he paused to shred small saplings before moving on. Several times during his morning travels he encountered does, and on two occasions

chased them a short distance before ending his pursuit. He was on a mission to find and breed an estrous doe.

Skies brightened by mid-morning, and every so often the sun's rays made their way to earth. It was still very cold, and the wind was picking up.

Near mid-day, the monarch bedded on a high spot along a ridgeline. His back was to the wind and he could see into the ravine below him. For the next 2 hours, he dozed. Sometimes he remained alert, and other times he stretched his head out flat on the ground in front of him. Even though his eyes were closed, his ears continued to monitor what was happening around him. On one occasion the danger signals from chattering squirrels brought him to full alert. It turned out to be a hawk looking for a meal.

Just as the buck was about to doze off again, he heard a branch break in the ravine below. He trained his eyes on the location of the sound. A doe and two fawns were heading up the ridge toward him. At 20 yards they scented him and stopped, cautiously examining the bedded buck. He stood and started toward them in a "bird-dog-trot." Wanting nothing to do with the buck, the

*Left: During this phase of the rut, rubbing will often be intense. I once observed a buck make four rubs over a 30-minute span, and all were within of 20 yards of each other.* **Right:** *Though rare, I've observed does rubbing existing buck rubs. Usually their rubbing is preceded by their smelling or licking the rub.*

*In areas with a good population of mature bucks, scraping behavior will be intense during this phase of the rut. Once the buck works the overhanging licking branch, it will paw the ground beneath then urinate over its tarsal glands, displaying a behavior called rub-urination.*

doe and fawns ran. The buck chased them for a short distance before stopping to smell the air. The scent of urine had grabbed his attention. He put his nose in the leaves and took as much scent as possible into his nasal cavity before raising his head and lip-curling. Ah, this was what he wanted! He sniffed around for the doe's trail and began tracking her.

For several hundred yards, the buck kept his nose glued to the ground, glancing up every so often to see where he was going. He came to a small clover field. In the center were two does,

three fawns and a dominant 8-point buck, similar in size to the big 10-pointer. The 8-pointer was trying to breed the doe, but with each pass he made at her, she moved off. The doe obviously was near estrus.

It takes two to tango, and three is a crowd in the deer world. Something serious was about to happen. The big 10-pointer emerged from the woods and approached the doe and buck with a stiff gait. The 8-pointer looked toward the 10-point and then back at the doe, which was now standing at the edge of the small clover field. With their hair bristling, the bucks moved toward each other. When the distance was cut to mere feet, they came together. For the next 2 minutes, they pushed and threw each other violently, tearing up the ground as they fought. The sound of antlers clashing filled the air. The 8-pointer proved to be too much for the big 10-point, and after being pushed to the ground, the 10-pointer broke away and ran for his life. At one point he felt the 8-pointer's tines ramming into his flank. After 100 yards he managed to enter the woods, at which point the other buck let him go.

With his ego marred, the big 10-point continued to walk. Nightfall was fast approaching and he still hadn't eaten anything all day. Along a ridgeline he came upon an area where acorns covered the ground. For the next half-hour he gorged himself in an attempt to catch up on the meals he had missed. After eating, he bedded under the canopy of several mature oaks. For the next 2 hours, he was content to lick his wounds and chew his cud.

By the time he felt like moving again it was totally dark. The winds had died and the forest was calm. Overhead, the sky was littered with hundreds of stars, along with half a moon. It was again time to look for does.

With only the moon and stars to light the way, the big buck exited the woods and walked into a cornfield. He stopped to assess the situation. He could hear corn stalks rustling nearby. Was it a doe or a buck? There was no breeze, so he couldn't smell what was there. He began easing through the rows of corn. His wide rack acted like a fish net and the long corn leaves began to tangle in his antlers. When he was just a short distance from the unidentified deer, it ran from him. It had to be a doe.

The big buck picked up the trail, which exited the field and went into nearby woods. More trailing, chasing, scraping and rubbing consumed the 10-pointer's next few hours. Feeling exhausted, the buck finally bedded. It had been a long day, but he knew that soon the does would stop running from him and he'd find the pot of gold at the end of the rainbow. He was about to have a part in the breeding season, which is what he lived for.

*Left:* Does often work a scrape's overhanging licking branch, though they seldom, if ever, paw the ground beneath. **Right:** Bucks often display aggressive chasing behavior when pursuing a doe, with such chases lasting for up to half an hour or more.

# CHAPTER 11

# Breeding Time

Unlike the seeking and chasing phases, does dictate the pace at which the breeding phase progresses. During the first two stages of the rut, bucks typically cover 4000 acres or more as they search for estrous does. However, they move much less once they have located a doe that is ready to breed. Because does generally cover only a quarter as much ground as bucks, overall deer movement often seems quite low once the seeking and chasing phases are complete and the breeding phase arrives.

Breeding marks the culmination of the rut. When a doe finally enters estrus, she will accept a buck's company wherever she goes. In many parts of North America, the doe-to-buck ratios are so weighted toward females that all bucks are able to find an estrous doe. When breeding begins, scraping nearly ceases and bucks curtail many of the activities they engaged in during the early portions of the rut.

The breeding phase usually begins about 7 days after the rutting moon (the second full moon after the autumnal equinox) and lasts approximately 14 days if the deer population is healthy and contains a sex ratio of no more than three adult does for every antlered buck. During this time, 70 to 80 percent of the mature does will likely be bred.

Rather than travelling, a buck will stay with a hot doe for up to 72 hours. For the first 24 hours, a doe will smell right but will not be ready to breed. During the second 24 hours, the doe will be in full estrus and will allow the buck to breed her several times (I once photographed a buck breeding a doe six times during an 8-hour period). Then, because she will continue to smell like she's in estrus for a third 24-hour period, the buck may continue to stay with her.

During the 3 days, the buck will move only when the doe moves. Because most does cover little ground, deer activity can seemingly halt during this time. Only when the doe cycles out of estrus will the buck move on to look for another female.

The first does to enter estrus will often cause a commotion by attracting several bucks. Seasoned hunters sometimes refer to this as a breeding party. When several bucks vie for the same doe, a dominant buck gets little rest as he tries to run off all intruding bucks in order to maintain his right to breed the doe. Because they have no time to rest or eat, it's not uncommon for dominant bucks to lose up to 25 percent of their body weight during the rut's seeking, chasing, and breeding phases.

Of all the stages of the rut, the breeding time can be the most difficult to hunt because movement is limited. At this point, tree stand hunters are likely to see deer only if their stands are located in areas frequented by doe groups.

## Doe Behavior

With a couple notable exceptions, a doe's life is pretty much the same during this phase of the rut as it was during the chasing phase. The exceptions are that does tend to be more active and urinate more prior to entering estrus. They also are more tolerant of bucks' advances.

Aside from these changes, does continue to go about their daily lives, bedding, feeding and staying within their family groups. When a doe enters estrus, a dominant buck almost always

*When two dominant bucks vie for the same doe, spectacular fights can result.*

*Breeding consumes every hour of a buck's life during the breeding phase of the rut. When a doe nears and enters estrus, a buck will hound her until breeding commences.*

drives off her fawns. Consequently, during the breeding window, her fawns can often be seen wandering aimlessly in the vicinity of the buck/doe courtship.

## Buck Behavior

As does enter estrus, bucks will cover much less ground, staying with the first breedable doe they locate. When they are no longer cruising their territory, scrapes go cold from lack of activity. This is especially true when an area has too many does relative to the number of antlered bucks.

The breeding process consumes every hour of a buck's life during this period. There is little time for food and rest, and diminished quantities of each take a heavy toll on bucks. In fact, there are recorded instances of dominant mature bucks succumbing to heart attacks due to the stress of the rut.

## A Day In the Life

With dawn breaking, the big 10-point emerged from an unharvested cornfield. There was a steady breeze blowing from the north, and the sky was spitting fine grains of snow. The smell of does floated on the wind. As the buck entered a wooded area that descended into a deep ravine, he paused to assess his surroundings. Far below, in the tangle of hemlocks and beech growth, he could hear the sound of deer running. Even though he was more than 100 yards away, the sounds of breaking branches, guttural grunts and snort-wheezes were well defined. A breeding party was in progress.

The big buck grunted twice before starting his descent into the ravine. It wasn't long before he came upon several deer scattered among a thick tangle of blowdowns along a dry streambed.

*Scraping will be intense right up to the breeding period. However, once the breeding begins, scraping behavior will nearly cease, with only a few scrapes remaining active.*

*During the breeding phase, bucks will make some impressive rubs, especially if they are pressured by other bucks for the right to breed a doe.*

All but one of the deer was milling around in the brush. Fifteen yards above the stream, a doe was standing, looking in the big buck's direction. As the 10-pointer approached, the doe turned to look off into the hardwoods. He paused, realizing that there was probably another deer nearby.

The doe bolted from her location above the buck and jumped the streambed in an attempt to flee a deer coming her way. It was a mature 8-point. Immediately, the big buck took up the chase, trying to cut off the other buck's approach. When the 8-pointer saw what was happening, he came to a screeching halt. It was obvious he was no match for the big 10-point. In a split second, everything came to a standstill. Every deer stood motionless, including the doe. Both bucks were standing and staring at each other from a distance of 15 yards.

The 10-point dropped his ears and aggressively snort-wheezed, dragging on the wheeze portion of the vocalization for several seconds. The 8-pointer's eyes drifted from the big buck to the doe standing 30 yards away. Before he could refocus on the 10-pointer, the big buck charged. The 8-point pivoted on his hind legs and narrowly escaped the ice-pick tines of the 10-point. The smaller buck ran without the 10-point following. After milling around for a couple minutes, the 8-pointer bedded just within sight of the doe. The woods calmed and the doe bedded in a thick tangle of treetops. The dominant buck approached and laid down less than 15 yards from her so he could guard her from the lingering 8-pointer.

For the next hour, the forest was silent. Then, amidst the chatter of blue jays and squirrels, something caught the 10-pointer's attention. He focused on a thick second-growth stand of hemlocks, 50 yards away. A deer emerged and stood motionless. It was a yearling 4-pointer.

In the opposite direction, the clatter of rocks in the dry streambed caused the big buck to jerk his head around to see the source of the noise. A 1½-year-old 6-point had come to survey the situation. The estrous doe was drawing a lot of attention. Now there were four bucks within 50 yards of her. Only one could do the breeding and the big 10-point had the right—or so he thought.

The 6-pointer didn't see the 10-point buck bedded near the doe, so he moved in. His gait resembled that of a dog moving in to point a bird. When the small buck cut his distance to 20 yards, his neck was stretched out so that his nose was barely off the ground. The thud, thud, thud sound of his hoofs touching the forest floor came closer and closer. The big 10-pointer decided the intruder had come far enough. Like a lightning

*Odors left at a rub site can be attractive to all deer. Both bucks and does will frequently lick freshly made rubs.*

*When two bucks engage in a knock-down-drag-out-fight, the sound can be heard for a long way. In addition to the sound of mashing antlers, snorting, grunting and bawling vocalizations will resonate from the battle area.*

bolt, he jumped to his feet, snort-wheezing as he rose. The yearling never knew what hit him. The dominant buck lowered his head and rammed the 6-point in the flank. At impact, the small buck moaned as he hurtled to the ground. Rising to his feet, he ran off through the woods with the big buck in hot pursuit.

Since the dominant buck was preoccupied, the 8-pointer rose from his bed and walked toward the doe. The 4-point yearling followed close behind. Just as they closed in on the doe, the big buck returned. He ran straight at the 8-point, which quickly changed direction, jumped a deadfall, and ran off.

With the 10-pointer chasing the 8-point buck, the yearling approached the doe. She jumped from her bed and began running up the side of the ravine with her two fawns in tow. Within seconds, the big buck returned and picked up the chase. As soon as the doe reached the top of the ravine, she bedded in a blowdown. The 4-pointer stopped and the big buck closed in on him quickly. Fearing for his life, the yearling wheeled to escape. With leaves flying and branches breaking underfoot, he retreated back into the ravine. He'd had enough.

The big 10-pointer stopped to catch his breath. Oxygen was hard to come by, and his body heaved as he tried to recover from all the running. It took a couple of minutes before the buck calmed down. He walked to within 15 yards of the bedded doe and then stood motionless, staring at her fawns 30 yards away.

One of the fawns began walking toward the bedded doe. Quickly, the 10-pointer snort-wheezed and moved in the direction of the fawn. He broke into a trot and ran off both of the fawns before returning to the doe. Breathing heavily again, the buck dropped to his knees and settled into a bedded position not far from her.

For the next hour the doe lay motionless, chewing her cud as the big buck watched her from his nearby bed. Every so often, he emitted a tending grunt, a continuous cadence of low grunts. During this time, the buck closed his eyes periodically as if he was sleeping. On one occasion, he laid his head flat on the ground as

he rested, only to come alert at the sound of a squirrel's warning chatter.

The doe rose to her feet. As she stretched, the buck jumped up as well. The doe walked from the blowdown and began feeding on acorns. The buck walked around the fallen tree to approach her. She looked back at him and he lowered his head, approaching her in the familiar bird-dog trot. She stood her ground and he proceeded to smell her and lick her flank. Slowly the big buck slid his jaw onto the doe's back and mounted her. Within 30 seconds, she was bred. The 10-point slid off the doe's back and stood next to her for a few moments. As he did, she occasionally looked at him from point-blank range.

With the buck standing motionless, the doe walked a few yards and began feeding. After consuming several acorns, she bedded again, this

*Nothing brings the helter-skelter rut to a grinding halt like the breeding phase. When a doe is in estrus, buck and doe may move only 100 yards in the course of a day. Only when the doe moves will the buck move.*

time in a more open area. The buck ate a few acorns and bedded as well.

Several hours passed before the bedded buck was again brought to alert. In the distance he could make out another deer coming his way. It was a big buck, about his size. The intruder's rack carried nine long points and his body language made it obvious that he smelled an estrous doe. He was about to crash the 10-pointer's party.

When the 9-point closed to within 30 yards, the 10-pointer rose to his feet. The newcomer stopped. For the next minute, the 10-point let out a series of snort-wheezes and tending grunts. A brawl was about to ensue.

The big 9-point slowly began walking toward the bedded doe, who was now looking over her shoulder at the approaching buck. Without hesitation, the big 10-pointer charged the 9-point. The doe scampered from her bed as the

**Left:** *Each time an estrous doe rises from her bed, she will walk a short distance and stop to wait for the breeder buck to approach her and breed.*

**Above:** *While an estrous doe rises to feed or move to re-bed, the dominant buck will be close to her side. During this time, the buck will often make a rub or scrape to solidify his dominance to any buck that is nearby.*

*When a doe finally enters estrus, she will tolerate the licking and grooming ritual of pair bonding. When this happens, breeding is imminent.*

two bucks collided 15 yards away. The woods had turned into a war zone. The mature bucks pushed each other back and forth. Small saplings collapsed under their weight. The sounds of branches breaking, antlers clashing together, and moaning and grunting were deafening. It was a fight to behold.

Two minutes into the fight, the bucks' antlers locked. They couldn't separate. With snow falling, they paused to catch their breath. Steam was rising from their backs. They remained motionless for a few seconds before continuing the struggle. Both bucks were nearly exhausted when the 10-point gained leverage and pushed the 9-pointer over a log. The 9-point lost his balance and the 10-point buck flipped over him, causing their antlers to unlock.

The 10-pointer now had the upper hand, and he thrust his big rack into his opponent's side. At

impact, the 9-point buck let out a deep moan. He struggled to his feet and attempted to run, but before he could escape the 10-pointer rammed him again. In spite of the wounds, the 9-pointer managed to run off through the woods.

Quiet returned to the forest. For the next half-hour the 10-point stood silently, trying to regain his strength after a hard-earned victory that had drained every bit of energy from him. Once he recovered, he began searching for the doe.

After trailing her for 500 yards, he came upon the doe and her fawns. They were bedded. With darkness falling, the buck bedded also. It had been a frenetic day.

During the next few hours, the 10-pointer ran off several bucks that tried to take the doe from him. None were big enough, though each caused the big buck to burn more energy—energy

*During the course of a doe's 24-hour estrous period, a buck may breed her six or more times.*

he didn't have. Throughout the night, he bred the doe four more times before she cycled out of estrus.

The following morning, with the smell of estrus no longer present, the mature 10-point rose from his bed near the doe and began walking. He didn't know where he was going, but he figured his nose would tell him soon enough. In spite of bruises, hunger pangs, and exhaustion, he marched on. He knew that somewhere within his territory there were more hot does. Until all of them had been bred, his mission would not be complete.

## Epilogue

I hope you've enjoyed my "day in the life" accounts in the last three chapters. No doubt some have never imagined that such behavior takes place in the whitetail's world. Had I not witnessed what I've written about many times over the last 30 years I might have doubts as well. However, I've lived every one of these experiences numerous times during my career. The events that unfold during the seeking, chasing and breeding phase of the rut are fascinating and an education beyond measure.

# CHAPTER 12

# Recovery Time

By the time the breeding phase of the rut starts to wind down, most bucks are a physical wreck. For the better part of 40 days, they have been chasing does and vying for breeding rights with other bucks. Though minor breeding activity will occur well into January in the North, bucks literally crash from physical exhaustion when December arrives in the northern part of the whitetail's range.

Many hunters and deer observers may challenge the notion that a buck's sex drive decreases in December. Granted, this often depends on the individual deer. However, research (Lambiase 1972) has shown that sperm production extends from mid-August through March for most bucks. The number of sperm per ejaculation typically increases through October, peaks in early November, nearly drops in half by mid-December, and declines at a slower rate thereafter. These facts demonstrate why bucks go into a rutting frenzy as the peak of the rut approaches around the middle of November. They also illustrate why the seeking, chasing and breeding phases of the rut are the best times to hunt sex-crazed bucks.

In addition, Lambiase's research shows why less rutting activity occurs in December, even though some does are in estrus. Mother Nature plays another card in this latter period. During November's peak rutting time, a buck's physical condition will progressively decline due to the rigors of the breeding ritual. Fat reserves are depleted, and in many cases, a buck will lose as much as 25-30 percent of his body weight by the time the rutting frenzy comes to an end.

## Survival Mode

A buck's ardor wanes after October and November. Rather than continuing to chase does, he will calm down and begin eating again in an attempt to regain the weight lost during the rut. Unfortunately, some bucks are unable to restore their depleted fat reserves. The subsequent winter and their remaining sex drive take a toll. Death claims many bucks, especially the most active breeders.

Because survival is the main objective, a buck becomes a different creature during December's post-rut recovery time. He will still breed, but he generally won't pursue does with the same intensity he showed in November. Instead, he will feed, rest and take what comes his way.

I've seen this scenario many times while photographing and hunting. When December arrives in the North, deer family groups begin to gravitate toward known food sources. In some cases, this might be a cornfield. In others, it's a cedar swamp that will soon serve as a yarding area. Regardless, bucks and does are intent on finding shelter and as much food as possible.

## Second Wind

I had an opportunity to observe the whitetail's recovery period firsthand in December 2002 while hunting in Saskatchewan. I arrived in this far-northern whitetail habitat on December 1, thinking I still might be able to observe some rutting behavior before the recovery period kicked in. I was wrong.

The first day of the hunt offered some hope as I saw 10 different bucks. None were chasing does; they were just cruising their territories. Then, on December 3, it seemed as if the rutting switch was turned off and the bucks were told to go to bed for a few days. By day four of the hunt, I realized what was taking place. Buck sightings were nearly non-existent for the remainder of my stay in Saskatchewan. The rut was over and it was

*A buck becomes a different creature during December's post-rut recovery time. Rather than trying to breed, he feeds and rests.*

I compare it to watching what happens to a marathon runner during the 2 days that follow this grueling 26-mile race. Most runners literally collapse as their bodies struggle to recover from the toll of the race. A very similar thing occurs with dominant whitetail bucks. If you are a hunter, the trick is to be in the woods just before or just after this period. If you find yourself hunting during this time frame, buck sightings will be hard to come by.

## A Second Rut?

In fine-tuned deer herds, the majority of breeding will be over by the time December's recovery period is in full swing. However, on good whitetail range where the herd is healthy and the fawns of the season are large enough, some December breeding will occur.

*By the time the recovery period arrives, bucks have lost up to 25 percent of their September body weight. Consequently, they must feed to regain critical fat reserves before winter sets in.*

*During the recovery period, bucks will bed for extended periods of time to recover from the exhaustion brought on by the rut.*

time for the bucks to catch their second wind and gear up for winter.

Had I not seen this scenario played out numerous times in other regions, I would have attributed the lack of buck sightings to other things. However, over the last 30 years, I've almost always witnessed a 5- to 7-day period at the end of the rut when bucks stay on their bellies, trying to recover from the rigors of the breeding season.

*Some breeding will occur well into January in the North. However, a buck does not search for estrous does. Rather, he takes what comes his way.*

In my area of western New York, many doe fawns that reach a body weight of 85-90 pounds by November will come into estrus and be bred sometime during December.

Most times, this "second rut" will be much more subdued than the November breeding period, but it still can cause a stir, especially if several bucks are in the area. On many occasions, I've watched this take place while photographing. During a recent December, I visited a known wintering area in the heart of New York's Adirondack Mountains with the intent of photographing some bucks before the severe cold of January. The snow had arrived in early December, and so had the deer. About 30 does and six bucks were in the area trying to bulk up on as much food as possible. On the second day of the photo shoot, it was obvious a doe was in estrus. The biggest buck in the area followed her around, but not aggressively. The other bucks, though at times interested, did not join in. They were more content to bed and feed.

Though the big buck finally bred the doe, he spent most of his time eating and resting. He occasionally gave a low, guttural grunt if another buck came too close, but he never showed aggressive behavior or engaged in any scraping activity. Only once did he rub a tree. It was almost as if the bucks knew the doe was ready to breed but didn't care which one of them did it.

Had it been mid-November, I can assure you the scene would have been far different.

## Return to Normal

Another of my experiences also typifies December deer activity. The day was December 9, and about 5 inches of snow covered the ground. In the morning, I hunted a blind overlooking a stream that runs through our farm. At about 10 a.m., I heard what sounded like deer chasing each other. Unfortunately, they were out of range and did not come closer. After an hour of silence, I headed home.

At about 3 p.m., with 2 hours of light remaining, I headed back to the area with my son, Aaron, who was 8 at the time. Fifteen minutes into our sit I heard two bucks sparring about 100 yards away. Minutes later, with the sparring still going on, four does moved down through the woods and out of sight. A 6-point buck followed them. Though the sparring grew louder and the bucks came closer, it wasn't aggressive.

With 20 minutes of light remaining, we spotted the four does coming back, with the yearling buck still in tow. All this time we listened to the bucks sparring, hoping they were larger than the yearling. The 6-pointer passed by and soon after, the other two bucks came into view and continued sparring in the small stream about 30 yards away.

Through my scope I could see one was a yearling and the other a heavy 6-pointer, probably a 2-year-old buck. Neither was big enough to harvest, so we sat and watched their every move. In the fading light, I brought my

*Though scraping behavior occurs during the recovery period, its intensity is but a fraction of what it was in October and November.*

grunt tube to my mouth and blew on it twice. At first the bucks ignored the sound, but two more grunts got their attention and the bigger buck started in our direction. At one point, he stood 15 paces in front of our ground blind, trying to figure out what had called. As darkness crept in, he turned and walked off to join his sparring partner.

Though these bucks exhibited a small amount of rutting activity, they had no interest in the four does that passed as they sparred. It was obvious they were more interested in roughhousing than sex. Again, had it been November, I'm sure they would have behaved differently.

## Sleep and Eat

During December's recovery time, sleeping and eating will dominate a whitetail's life, with the locations of food sources dictating where deer bed and sleep. Unlike November, when bucks are observed on the prowl throughout the day, December finds the majority of deer bedded. It's not uncommon for deer to bed over 75 percent of the time when they are recovering from the rut. Typically a whitetail will bed for 2-4 hours during this time before getting up and moving around. Sometimes a deer will do little more than stretch and relieve itself when it rises from its bed. On other occasions, it might browse on nearby vegetation for a while and then rebed.

It's been my experience that the majority of daytime activity during the December recovery period occurs at mid-day and during the last 2

*Throughout the post-rut period, all whitetails will try to gorge themselves on available food supplies before winter arrives. During this time, they may consume up to 7 pounds of food a day.*

hours before sunset. During these two stretches of activity, deer can be found trying to gorge themselves on any preferred foods that are available.

In the heavily forested regions of the country, browse from maple, oak, ash, basswood and hemlock are a few of the foods deer will gravitate to at this time of the year. In farm country, standing cornfields and clover and alfalfa plots will be their food sources of choice.

The volume of food consumed by a whitetail during the post-rut recovery period will vary according to the needs of the individual animal and the availability of preferred foods. Over the years, food intake by the whitetails I've raised has averaged 7 to 9 pounds per animal per day. This is less than they consume during the prime antler-growing months of the summer but significantly more than the amount required during the winter.

**Top:** *During the recovery period, some rubs will be made. From this point on, rubbing behavior will decrease until antler casting takes place.* **Bottom:** *In farm-country regions, the range of bucks during the recovery period will be less than half what it was in the rut. Few deer will cover over 1000 acres when the colds of winter arrive.*

# CHAPTER 13

# Season of Endurance – Winter

Snow had been falling constantly for 2 days. It was the beginning of December, and I was in New York's Adirondack Mountains attempting to do some early-winter photography. I eased my vehicle through the slippery curves of Route 10. Heavy snow clung to the evergreens along the roadside, weighing down their branches to the breaking point. It was truly a winter wonderland.

Rounding a bend, I saw two deer standing in the middle of the snowy highway. Within seconds of our encounter they bolted, jumped the snow bank and vanished into the forest. I slowed to get a look at them, but snow cover kept me from seeing anything. Nearly stopped, I turned my head to the other side of the road. There, 20 yards into the woods, stood four other deer. As I crept by, they ran across the road behind me to follow the other two. It was only then that I noticed several heavily worn trails that crossed the road. The whitetail's winter migration had begun, and I was right in the middle of it.

Winter throughout the whitetail range is incredibly varied. Though its impact on southern whitetails may not be great, the stress it piles on northern deer is significant. Harsh weather usually arrives by mid-December in the North. For the next 3 to 4 months, whitetails are subjected to ice, freezing rain, severe cold and snow, with snow depths exceeding 4 feet in some areas.

*Where significant snow depth occurs, a situation called yarding takes place, where deer bunch up and gravitate toward traditional food sources and cover.*

I consider myself very fortunate to have lived my entire life in the northern reaches of the whitetail's range. For the better part of 50 years, I've watched deer struggle to survive the cold and snow. This is never a pretty thing to see, but the experience has given me a tremendous appreciation for the whitetail's resilience and will to survive. It is an incredibly opportunistic and resourceful creature.

To survive winter's fury, God made northern whitetails much larger than their southern cousins. By way of example, Margarita Island, which lies off the coast of Venezuela, is home to white-tailed deer that tip the scales at around 40 pounds as adults. Mature whitetail bucks found near the 52nd latitude in Canada can have a live weight of about 400 pounds. This phenomenon is referred to as Bergmann's Rule, after the scientist who first observed that body size generally increases with latitude. Larger bodies make northern whitetails better equipped to survive harsh winters.

Nothing takes a greater toll on whitetails than winter. Heavy snow, severe cold and shortage of food often cause whitetail herds to teeter on the brink of disaster. In portions of the North, the annual winter death toll has been known to exceed the number of deer harvested by

*Nothing takes a greater toll on Northern whitetails than winter. In severe years, some Northern deer ranges will get 200-300 inches of snowfall.*

# Yarding

In many areas north of the 40th latitude, whitetails typically begin migrating when the snows of December arrive. Though most herds will go less than 2 or 3 miles, some whitetails will move up to 30 miles as they migrate to their winter range. Once they arrive at their wintering area, they will stay put for up to 120 days.

Where significant snow depth accumulates, "yarding" occurs. This term refers to deer bunching up and gravitating toward sources of food and cover. Unfortunately, the food in many traditional yarding areas was depleted long ago, making it impossible for whitetails to find their daily requirement of 6 pounds of browse.

In remote areas like Michigan's Upper Peninsula, New York's Adirondack Mountains, or Maine's famed Allagash region, whitetails begin migrating to their familiar wintering areas when the heavy snows begin. Such

*No food source is overlooked by whitetails during the winter months. This buck can be seen feeding on lichens growing on the bark of a tree.*

hunters during the course of the year. The 120 days between mid-December and mid-April can be an endurance test for deer in the North. In the most severe situations, some northern deer ranges will receive 200-300 inches of snowfall. In my home state of New York, the Tug Hill area off the eastern end of Lake Ontario has been known to get over 7 feet of snowfall in less than 72 hours when lake effect snow bands develop. It's hard to imagine how deer survive when this happens, but they do.

locations are usually large conifer swamps that offer protection against winter's cold. These "yards," with their thick cover, allow deer to conserve energy and protect them from winds and predators.

Winter is quite different in farm country. For the most part, there is little or no migration. The only thing resembling a migration occurs when a local herd moves from a north-facing area to a south-facing location. This usually results in a relatively small 2- or 3-mile shift.

*If available, all whitetails will heavily browse tree branches. In the Northeast, browse like aspen, sumac, red maple, basswood and white cedar are preferred foods. Their food requirement during winter is about 5-7 pounds of food per day.*

## Food Requirement

It's tough for a whitetail to make a living during the winter months. On most northern ranges, the food required to maintain a whitetail's body is not available. Consequently, most deer must live off their fat reserves.

A biological shift within all whitetails occurs as they adjust to winter. During the early part of the season, they have reduced thyroid function and decreased metabolic activity. This results in less food being needed for survival. Then by mid-winter, they slow down even further, entering a state in which they are almost hibernating on the hoof. Scientists refer to this as semi-hibernation.

It allows deer to become quite resistant to nutritional deprivation and the stresses of winter's harsh climate. This phenomenon reduces a deer's food intake by approximately 30 percent, regardless of the food available, and causes activity to fall by up to 50 percent.

The downside of semi-hibernation is that deer become very reluctant to move from one location to another in search of new sources of food. I've seen this behavior exhibited often when I've gone into a particular wintering area to photograph or cut browse. During tough winters, I've had to cut trees within 300 yards of where the deer were bedding just to get them interested in the new supply of food. Other times I've seen deer within a half a mile of an excellent food source show little interest in going to it. This almost gave me the impression that the food had to be right under their noses before they would bother with it. This tendency to stay in a relatively small area can make it difficult for whitetails to get 6 or 7 pounds of browse each day, which is the amount they require for survival.

If whitetails happen to spend the winter where the habitat has been damaged or good food is not present, their condition deteriorates quickly. For this reason, it's important for them to winter where more nutritional foods are available. In the Northeast, browse like aspen, sumac, red maple, basswood, apple, white ash, white cedar and hemlock are preferred foods and are vital to a herd's survival. When northern whitetails begin feeding on non-preferred foods like American beech and striped maple, it's an indication they are in trouble.

Though whitetails are very sluggish during the winter months, they can be very aggressive toward each other when food is involved. Many times while photographing I've seen deer fight each other for food, or guard a given source of browse they've found. Such displays are not pretty sights, especially when a doe competes with her fawns for nourishment. Winter truly is a time of survival of the fittest.

## Antler Casting

Range condition, nutrition availability, genetics, testosterone levels, and overall health are all factors that help to determine when a buck will cast his antlers. In most northern climates, the casting or shedding of antlers takes place from December to March. Popular literature suggests that the older, more mature bucks drop their antlers first. I've found this to be true where rut-worn bucks inhabit an area with marginal food sources. However, in locations where food is abundant, I've seen trophy-class bucks carry their antlers into late March.

I've witnessed a definite genetic influence in the casting times of bucks I've raised. When a buck's nutritional requirement is met and he doesn't have to breed too many does, he will cast his antlers at nearly the same time each year. Several of the bucks I've raised have consistently shed their antlers within 2 or 3 days of a certain date every year.

*When the snows of winter arrive, autumn and its abundance are replaced with cold and food shortages. From mid-December to March, most Northern deer herds are in crisis mode.*

# Bedding Behavior

Whitetails bed for two reasons: to rest and to be in a better position to survive. From birth, deer learn to survive by keeping a low profile in the cozy confines of their bedding area. It's in these places that they chew, doze, groom and pass the day away as they struggle for the chance to see another sunrise.

For the most part, they know they are in danger every time they begin to move. Consequently, they remain bedded most of the day during the winter months. Scientists have calculated that deer often bed 90 percent of the time in the winter. Part of the reason for this is that bedding conserves energy, allowing deer to ward off cold-stress. However, in years when temperatures are below normal and snow depth is above average, cold-stress can be a real death warrant, especially to the youngest and oldest members of the whitetail population.

Nearly three decades ago, Cornell University researcher Dr. Aaron Moen documented that a whitetail's heart beats 72 times per minute when bedded, 86 times per

*If doe fawns of the year can attain weights of 80 or more pounds by November, some will breed in December and January, creating what some refer to as a "second rut." In reality, the cold of winter and other factors reduce this to little more than a minor event.*

minute when standing, 102 times per minute when walking, and more than 155 times per minute when running. So, in the dead of winter, whitetails can conserve a lot of energy by remaining inactive.

The length of time a whitetail beds depends on a host of factors. A deer's age and health, the time of year, weather conditions, and pressure from predators are all parts of the equation. On average, most deer will not bed longer than 2 hours. An exception to this occurs in the far-northern reaches of the whitetail's range. Where intense snow and cold persist, I've seen deer

*To rid themselves of falling snow, all deer will periodically shake themselves.*

remain bedded for up to 6 hours at a time without rising and moving around. Scientists have concluded that when air temperatures drop below 10 degrees Fahrenheit or when a combination of cold and strong winds prevails, deer will bed for extended periods of time, in some cases 24 hours or more.

After bedding, deer will often stand, stretch and bed again in the same place. Other times, they will walk anywhere from a few yards to several hundred yards to feed or bed again.

## Buck Behavior

A buck's age, health, personality, level of dominance over other males in his core area, and the amount of environmental stress he experiences will dictate the type of behavior he exhibits during the winter season. Once the rut is over, bucks will either migrate to yarding areas or return to their core range. They also reform bachelor groups similar to those that develop during the summer months. When not bedded or feeding, a buck will often interact with other bucks in his group. This interaction takes on the form of grooming and sparring. The latter is especially common among the subordinate bucks within a bachelor group.

As during other times of the year, bucks will seldom occupy the same immediate area as does in the winter. They have their own core areas and remain separated from females, except when their feeding and travel patterns cause them to cross paths.

Bucks will also exhibit various rutting behaviors during the winter months. Though scraping will not occur like it does during the fall,

*During the winter months, testosterone levels plummet and bucks reform bachelor groups. During this time, grooming among bucks can be quite common.*

bucks will occasionally work a scrape's overhanging licking branch. I've photographed this behavior often, and although it's not uncommon for a buck to feverishly work a licking branch, he'll seldom paw the ground beneath it.

With testosterone levels at low ebb, antler rubbing is much less intense than during the autumn. How often bucks rub their antlers during the winter months is frequently debated among hunters. My experience from photography and hunting is that a buck will rub even after he casts his antlers. When rubbing behavior takes place in the winter, its intensity and length are minimal.

Of all rutting behaviors exhibited during the winter months, sparring is probably the most common. Yearling and subordinate bucks frequently engage in sparring behavior, right up to the time they cast their antlers. A common sparring behavior I've witnessed and photographed in wintering areas involves a buck walking over to a bedded buck and sparring with him while he is still bedded. I've seen such encounters last anywhere from 30 seconds to 10 minutes.

## Doe Behavior

Once the rut is over and winter sets in, does return to a buckless world. They pretty much keep to themselves, opting to live within their core family groups. Like bucks, they will be bedded the majority of the time during winter, rising only to feed or change their bedding locations.

If it wasn't for the hyperactive nature of fawns, I'm convinced that doe sightings would be much less frequent than they are during the winter months. Through photography, I've been able to observe the way fawns interact with their mothers during the winter. Often, the behavior is almost comical. Unlike does, fawns cannot stay still, so they are constantly up and down, moving around and sometimes pestering their mothers. Occasionally, the doe will give in, get up, and begin moving around as well.

Last year while photographing in a wintering area, I witnessed two fawns in what appeared to be a tag-team pestering match with their mother. First one would get up, walk over to the bedded doe, and lick and nudge her. When the doe seemed to ignore this routine, the fawn would return to its bed, only to have its sibling get up and do the same thing. After about a half-hour of repeated harassment, the doe got up and moved off through the brush with the fawns in tow. There was no doubt that she wanted to rest and conserve energy, but the fawns wouldn't let her.

Temperature has much to do with deer activity during the winter months. If temperatures are below the norm for an area, deer sightings will be scant. If they are normal or above average, both bucks and does will be moving around, looking for food.

## Predation

In addition to starvation, northern whitetails also must cope with the constant threat of predation. They are susceptible to coyotes, wolves and domestic dogs during the winter months, when their strength is at its lowest. In many areas of the North, predation is considerable, especially when snow depth is significant.

Winter-stressed deer in deep snow are no test for packs of coyotes or wolves. Domestic dogs that have the benefit of returning to their home each day for food and shelter can wreak havoc on deer living in populated areas. During late winter, dogs can run on top of the crust that forms on the snow and easily catch deer that try to flee but break through the crust.

*During the early part of winter, whitetails have reduced thyroid function and decreased metabolic activity. Consequently, over 90 percent of their time is spent bedded. Scientists refer to this as semi-hibernation.*

# CHAPTER 14

# Cast to Cast

This series of photos documents the antler growth and behavior of a buck I photographed over the course of 10 years. The buck lived on an incredible piece of property in the Northeast that was off limits to hunting. Aside from protection from hunters, he had a normal life, complete with many challenges from Mother Nature. His home range featured a substantial predator population and received significant snowfall during the harsh winter months.

As mentioned earlier, I've been able to imprint many whitetails on the sound of corn rattling in a plastic can. This particular buck was one such animal. Unlike many of the deer on this particular property, the buck had a gentle disposition and never exhibited any aggressiveness toward me, even during the full-blown rut. Consequently, I was able to follow him and document some incredible behavior over a period of several years. As the buck aged, I was even able to feed him out of my hand.

Interestingly, this buck was only a 3-inch spike as a yearling. His largest set of antlers was grown in his 6th year and measured 167 Boone and Crockett. Once the buck reached 4 years of age, he began casting his antlers on nearly the same day each year. This allowed me to know when I needed to be present in order to capture these rare antler-casting images. Only once did the buck shed both antlers at the same time. Normally, he would cast one antler around February 25 each year and then carry the other for a day or two.

This particular sequence was taken when the buck was 7 years old. It covers a full year in his life—from antler cast to antler cast. During the year these photos were taken, his rack scored 165 Boone and Crockett.

# Winter

The sequence begins in the dead of winter, a time the Native Americans referred to as the "Hunger Moon." In the area this buck lived, it's not uncommon for temperatures to hover between zero and the low teens for days on end. Such bitter cold is the reason the natural world comes to a halt in the North during January and February.

During the year this sequence was photographed, this buck was in the prime of his life. He was the dominant buck in the area, and with the exception of occasional interaction with the other bucks in his bachelor group, he kept to himself during the winter. About 90 percent of his time was spent bedded, with his daytime feeding usually taking place at mid-day and during the last hour of daylight. In spite of snow depths in excess of one foot for most of the winter, he appeared to come through March in very good shape.

*The buck in this photo essay was only a 3-inch spike as a yearling. His largest set of antlers was grown in his sixth year and measured 167 Boone and Crockett points.*

# February 25

*With the buck's testosterone level bottomed out, he casts his last antler on February 25. Within hours, the blood on the antler pedicle dries and scabs over. By March 20, the buck's antlers begin growing again.*

# Spring

As with most mature bucks I've observed over the years, this buck began growing his antlers around the 20th of March. His antler growth was minimal during the first month. However, when spring green-up arrived and the days became longer, his antler growth accelerated. When winter passed its torch to spring, the big buck's changing fur coat made him look very unhealthy. Like the other deer in the area, he began losing clumps of fur around the first of May. By the beginning of June, his summer coat was fully-grown and he took on a very sleek look.

When June bursts on to the scene, black flies and other insects become a real nuisance for wildlife. Consequently, the latter stages of spring can be very stressful for northern whitetails. This buck attempted to flee the insects' assaults by bedding in high grass and staying close to water sources. As a result, he was often hard to locate later in the spring.

## May 1

*By May 1, the buck's antlers are 4 inches long and sport brow tines. Also, the buck's summer coat is replacing his winter coat at this point.*

# June 1

n June 1 arrives, antler growth is beginning to explode. The buck's antlers now sport 6 points. With vegetation and day length about to
he begins encountering stress from insects and heat.

## Summer

By the time July arrived, the buck was beginning to show his antler potential. Though they would eventually be much longer, all of his antler points were visible by mid-July. He also became more predictable as the summer progressed, and I often photographed him in a couple different clover fields at either end of the day. He would feed alone occasionally, but it was more common for him to stay in a bachelor group of four bucks, of which he was the largest.

By August 1, his antlers were full-grown and were as big as they would be at any point during the year. Around mid-August, they began to shrink in size, and the velvet on them changed from a dark brown color to a grayish tone that is typical when the antler calcification process begins.

I photographed the buck just before dark on September 4, and it didn't appear that his antlers were ready to peel. However, when I located him the following day, he had stripped almost all of the velvet from his rack.

## July 15

*By mid-July, the mature buck is sleek and his antlers are nearly full-grown. During the summer months, bucks are very secretive, bed a great deal and move only at the edges of day.*

# August 20

*The buck's antler growth is now complete, and his winter coat is starting to replace his summer coat. Within days, the velvet covering on his antlers will crack and be peeled.*

## Autumn

As autumn progressed, the big 9-pointer revealed his dominance to the bucks in the area at every opportunity. He would do this by staring down other bucks, dropping his ears, bristling his hair and, in a few cases, fighting. Because he was the largest buck around, most of the others never challenged him to a fight.

During September and October, the buck didn't move a great deal during daylight, preferring to feed at either end of the day. By the latter part of September, he no longer spent time with his summer bachelor group, opting instead to keep to himself. Frequently, I photographed him making rubs and scrapes.

By the end of October he was in peak condition and laden with fat. He also was becoming increasingly active. When the air temperature dropped below 40 degrees, I knew he would be up and moving around his territory. During one 2-hour period I photographed him making 10 scrapes and two rubs. He had turned into a rutting machine. By the time the rutting moon shown full on November 4, he looked like he was ready to explode. During the week that followed, he challenged every buck and chased every doe he encountered. He also vocalized a great deal. It was obvious from his aggressive behavior that his testosterone had peaked.

On November 18, the weather turned cold and the season's first snowfall arrived. Bucks were going ballistic, including the big 9-pointer. He had found a doe near estrus and stuck close to her side. Throughout the day, three smaller bucks stayed close enough to cause quite a commotion. Their presence highly irritated the big buck. He trashed small trees, snort-wheezed and tried to run them off. Because they knew the doe was nearing estrus they hung around in spite of the big 9-pointer's challenges. This scenario continued for two days.

On November 19, I photographed the big buck breeding the doe four times during the course of the day. By midday on the 20th, the doe obviously had cycled out of estrus and no longer "smelled right," as the buck left her to look for another breeding opportunity.

## September 5

*Shorter days trigger a hormone change in bucks. Increased levels of testosterone cause antlers to harden and bucks to shed their velvet. On September 5, the peeling process begins. In a span of 24 hours, the buck removes all of the velvet from his antlers.*

*When autumn's shorter days arrive, bucks will go into a rutting frenzy by making rubs and scrapes throughout their territory.*

*Throughout the fall, subordinate bucks continually challenge the big buck's dominance. At times, the fights that result are quite spectacular.*

# November 18

*On the 18th of November, the buck is greeted with the season's first snowfall and a doe coming into estrus.*

# November 20

*On November 20, after pair-bonding for over 24 hours, the doe allows the buck to breed her. During daylight on the 20th, I observe the buck breeding the doe four times.*

## Winter

By early December, the buck appeared to have lost a considerable amount of weight from the rut. He was no longer looking for does. Instead, he spent much of his time bedding and feeding. His winter routine had returned.

Because this buck lived on excellent range and had access to ample food, he always dropped his antlers within a day or two of the previous year beginning when he was 4 years old. Consequently, he shed one antler on February 23rd and two days later the other was cast. His yearly cycle was complete.

## February 23

*The big buck casts his first antler on February 23. On February 25, his right antler drops, completing the cast-to-cast sequence.*

# CHAPTER 15

# Biology

Today, the white-tailed deer numbers over 30 million and is the most plentiful big-game animal in North America, with 30 recognized subspecies. These various subspecies inhabit land from the equator to the 52nd parallel in Canada. The body sizes of these subspecies vary greatly. Generally, the farther north one goes, the larger the whitetails are. This is reflected in the Northern Woodland and Dakota subspecies, which are the largest.

*Whitetail country spans America. There are over 30 million whitetails in North America, with 30 recognized subspecies.*

## Body Vitals

*Size and weight:* In the northern reaches of the whitetail's range, a mature buck will be about 42 inches tall at the shoulder, while in the southernmost region, a buck will be little more than half as tall. In many parts of North America, bucks that weigh over 250 pounds cause a great deal of excitement. Deer of this size will field dress (vital organs removed) just over 200 pounds. Though the 200-pound threshold seems to be a benchmark for big bucks, several field dressing over 300 pounds have been recorded.

In November of 1955, Horace Hinkley shot the heaviest buck ever officially recorded in Maine. The buck, from the Northern Woodland subspecies, had a field-dressed weight of 355 pounds, which means that its live weight was in excess of 400 pounds. It appears that the heaviest whitetail ever killed in the United States was taken by Minnesota hunter Carl Lenander, Jr. in 1926. It field-dressed at 402 pounds, and the state conservation department estimated the buck's live weight to be 511 pounds.

Perhaps the heaviest whitetail of all fell to archer John Annett of Ontario, Canada, in 1977. It field-dressed 431 pounds on government

## Ranges of Whitetail Subspecies

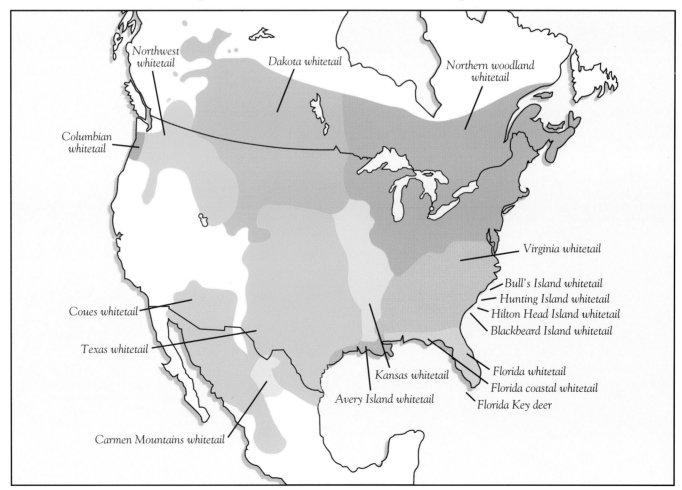

Northwest whitetail

Dakota whitetail

Northern woodland whitetail

Columbian whitetail

Coues whitetail

Texas whitetail

Carmen Mountains whitetail

Kansas whitetail

Avery Island whitetail

Virginia whitetail

Bull's Island whitetail

Hunting Island whitetail

Hilton Head Island whitetail

Blackbeard Island whitetail

Florida whitetail

Florida coastal whitetail

Florida Key deer

*Top:* In many portions of North America, mature bucks can grow impressive antlers. I photographed this buck in the fertile farmland of Ohio. His antlers will easily score over 230 Boone and Crockett. **Bottom:** A buck will almost always need to be over 4½ years old to grow a set of antlers this size. It's hard to believe that such antlers are grown in about 110 days, but they are.

certified scales. Unfortunately, the deer was processed before Canadian authorities could examine it.

Northern females are considerably smaller than males. Within the Dakota and Northern Woodland subspecies, it is rare to have an adult doe with a live weight exceeding 175 pounds.

In contrast to their larger cousins in the North, whitetails found near the equator in Central America may reach live weights of 40-70 pounds.

*Antlers:* Though some states consider weight to be the key ingredient in determining how big a whitetail is, antlers are at the heart of the whitetail's popularity and are viewed by hunters as the ultimate measure of whether a buck is considered a trophy. A 1½-year-old buck will generally vary from a spike to a small 8- or 10-point. Older bucks, in the age class ranging from 3½ to 7½ years, may carry trophy antlers with 8 or more points.

In the last two decades, more hunters have become knowledgeable about the Boone and Crockett scoring system and what it takes to grow a trophy-class whitetail buck. For over 80 years, Jim Jordan's 10-point Wisconsin buck stood as the largest typical whitetail ever killed, scoring 206⅛ Boone and Crockett points. Then, in November of 1993, Milo Hanson of Bigger, Saskatchewan, harvested a huge 14-point buck that scored 213⅛ typical.

It is generally accepted that a 140-class Boone and Crockett whitetail is a true trophy, regardless of where it is found. For a whitetail to be able to grow 140 inches of antler, it usually needs to be at least 3½ years old. Though a buck may sport a trophy set of antlers at 3½ years of age, he doesn't reach full maturity until age 5½ or 6½. With proper genetics and habitat, a 5½-year-old buck can easily grow a rack that will score in the range of 160-175 typical.

In recent years, there has been much discussion regarding the fact that some whitetail bucks have dark antlers while others grow very light-colored racks. Some well-known experts have stated that the variation in antler color is based on factors such as a buck's genetics, the region of the country in which he lives and the vegetation on which he rubs his antlers. Having raised many bucks and traveled to various parts of the country to photograph and hunt, it's my feeling that there are probably several factors that determine antler coloration, with perhaps the biggest being genetics. I base this on experience, what I've read in popular literature, and the fact that, of the nine whitetail bucks I'm currently raising, two are dark-antlered, two carry medium to dark headgear, and five have very light-colored racks. All rub on the same vegetation. This seems to point to genetics as a significant contributor to antler coloration.

*Life span:* If whitetails could live without predators and have access to ample food, most could be expected to live 10 to 12 years relatively

*During the early days after velvet peel, bucks will be in bachelor groups. However, as their testosterone levels rise and the rut approaches, the groups will break up. During the rut, bucks will often cover over 4000 acres in their pursuit of does.*

*Throughout most of the year, does will live separate from bucks. Only during the rut will they be found in close proximity to each other.*

The oldest known whitetail buck is well documented. The deer, named Henry II, lived to be 20 years and 9 months. He was owned by a personal friend of mine, whitetail breeder Ben Lingle of Clearfield, Pennsylvania. The buck was raised in captivity and grew his largest set of antlers when he was 15 years old. That year, his rack scored nearly 170 Boone and Crockett.

easily. Unfortunately, there is no utopia in the world of the whitetail. Many factors play a role in how long a deer lives. One of the critical factors in determining a deer's longevity is the condition of its teeth. When age-related wear becomes a problem, many health problems usually follow.

In most parts of North America, particularly the Northeast, over 75 percent of all whitetail bucks are killed when they are 1½ years old, and very few bucks ever reach their prime, which is 4½ to 5½ years of age.

Because males are so competitive, does tend to fare much better than bucks, both in the wild and in captivity. Though detailed records are sketchy, there seems to be some evidence that the oldest whitetail doe on record lived in captivity in Putney, Vermont. The doe lived to be 19½ years old.

**Ranging habits:** The amount of territory whitetails cover within their range varies throughout North America. In big timber country like northern Saskatchewan, the Adirondack Mountains of New York, and Maine's Allagash region, rutting whitetail bucks will cover well over 4000 acres.

One of the best deer trackers in North America is Maine's Dick Bernier. Bernier tracks big bucks in northern Maine, and on many occasions he has tracked a buck over 15 miles in a day, only to find the same buck back at the previous day's starting point the following morning. "Mileage means nothing to big rutting bucks because they have doe groups they check over and over during the rut," Bernier said. "These doe groups are sometimes so spread out that the buck will have to cover more than 15 miles in a day to check them. Understand that this is usually not 15 miles in a straight line, but rather 15 miles of travel within a 5-square-mile area. To survey his area a buck does a lot of zigzagging, and in doing so he will often cover 15 miles in a day."

In prime agricultural areas where the doe population is high, a buck's range may be less than 4000 acres. During non-rutting months, bucks are often very reclusive and usually cover less than 1000 acres.

Does, on the other hand, will seldom cover more than 1000 acres once they've established their home range. Telemetry studies have shown that during fawning times, some does stay for weeks on end in wood and brush lots that are less than 50 acres in size if cover and food are readily available.

## Athleticism

Few animals on God's green earth have the athletic ability to rival a whitetail. This is one of the reasons it has been able to survive and thrive better than other members of the deer family.

Whitetails are capable of running at speeds up to 40 miles per hour in the open and nearly as fast in forest settings. Though they cannot sustain

**Inset:** *In some regions of the country, biologists are able to determine deer populations by the density of deer feces.*
**Bottom left and right:** *Whitetails are incredible athletes. They can easily jump 6-feet-high deadfalls and fences.*

these speeds for long periods of time, they still are fast enough to flee many of their predators.

Along with their speed, whitetails are blessed with the ability to bound up to 30 feet at time and jump over high fences. In the process of raising deer, I've observed that if they attempt to jump an 8-foot-high fence, they normally hit it at about the 7-foot mark. Though I have never personally watched it take place, I've had people tell me they've seen a deer clear an 8-foot fence. For this to happen, everything must be in the deer's favor, from the angle of the land to a

jumping site that is open and allows the deer to gain the speed necessary for a strong launch. Regardless of whether they can jump 7, 8 or 10 feet high, whitetails' ability to leap tall obstacles is very impressive considering their average shoulder height of 35 to 42 inches.

## Senses

The white-tailed deer's ability to process sensory information is incredible. Dennis Olson, author of *Way of the Whitetail*, sums it up best: "Of course, we value intellect as the trait of 'higher' animals. Deer are long on instinct and short on our version of logic. They are rather stupid compared to computers, satellites, complicated business deals, and us. But, if just once we could let deer design an IQ test, the first question might be which odors on the wind right now are edible, which are dangerous, and which are neutral? Who flunks that test?" Olson's assessment says much about how the whitetail uses its senses to survive.

**Smell:** Deer live in a world of scent, and of all their defense mechanisms, their olfactory senses are the most important. As incredible as its other senses are, the whitetail's ability to decipher smells and sort out danger is legendary. Depending on which "expert" you talk to, you'll get a number of different answers as to how well a whitetail can smell. Some say they can smell 100 times better than humans, while others feel it is closer to 1000 or 10,000 times greater.

Over the years, I've had the opportunity to discuss the whitetail's ability to smell with several well-known scientists. Though much of it is a mystery, scientists know that a large portion of

*By November, fighting is quite common as bucks vie for territorial and breeding dominance.*

the whitetail's nasal interior is lined with a skin called epithelium, which is covered with a mucous membrane. It's here that thousands of scent receptors are located. The epithelium in a larger deer will have a greater surface area, so older deer generally are able to smell better than younger deer.

If you were to cross-section a whitetail's nose, you'd notice that it is quite long and has a scroll-like structure of bones and membranes inside the nasal passage. A scientist once told me that this area of a whitetail's nose has 100 times more surface area than a human's nose. He went on to say that a whitetail's sense of smell is so much greater than that of a human because the sensitive nerve endings in this region of its nose are so well developed. He surmised that it wasn't unthinkable to assume that, under certain circumstances—namely damp conditions—a whitetail could smell over 1000 times better than humans.

During my speaking engagements, I'm often asked how good a deer's sense of smell is. I respond by sharing an experience from raising deer. My whitetail research facility is 35-acres in size and lies in the center of our farm. During November, when the wind blows into the enclosure, my bucks often camp out along the fence facing into the wind. They do this because they can smell the does bedded outside the enclosure. What is

*A whitetail's sense of smell is legendary. Many experts believe they can smell 100 times better than humans.*

interesting is that the enclosure's southern fence is 425 yards from the nearest wooded area. Even at that distance, the bucks will stand at the fence, looking across the open expanse to the woods. They can't see any deer from that distance, but they certainly can smell them.

Whether whitetails can smell 100 or 1000 times better than humans will probably always be open for discussion. The bottom line is that their sense of smell is so acute that very little goes undetected.

*Eyesight:* When I took my first hunter safety course as a kid, I remember hearing a local game warden say that whitetails were color blind and could only see in shades of black and white. At the time, I wondered how this could be. As I grew older, other "experts" echoed a similar mantra. Only in the last several years has this theory been disproved.

Researchers at the University of Georgia have concluded that whitetails have the necessary cone cell structure in their eyes to see certain colors. Because of this, it's believed that deer can probably see in two different wavelengths of color. They appear to have very good vision in the blue range of the color spectrum, which allows them to see in very low or dim light. This explains their apparent ability to see well at night. They also can undoubtedly see in the mid-range spectrum of yellow. Two colors they apparently cannot see are red and green.

In January of 2000, with 8 inches of snow on the ground, I ran an experiment in our whitetail facility to determine just how well deer can see. I took red and yellow apples and placed them in a row 40 yards long, roughly 10 feet apart. The apples were placed so the deer could see them but not smell them when they came to the feeding area. In every instance, the deer went to the yellow apples first. They appeared to be able to find the red apples only if they could smell them first. The red apples probably appeared gray to the deer and blended in with the snow, while the yellow apples were easily seen because of whitetails' ability to detect the yellow range of the color spectrum. This simple experiment seemed to support the research done at the University of Georgia.

Though deer see colors a bit differently than people, most experts agree that they can see as well or better than humans. They may fall short of us in detecting stationary objects from a distance. However, their ability to detect an object with even the slightest movement is considered excellent.

***Hearing:*** Though a whitetail's hearing ability doesn't get as much attention as its ability to smell, it should. Time and time again, I've witnessed the whitetail's incredible hearing. It's been my experience that a deer's ability to hear far exceeds that of a human.

This is better understood through the writings of legendary whitetail expert Dr. Leonard Lee Rue III, who summarizes the whitetail's ability to hear as follows: "The auditory canal openings in deer and humans are the same size, about one-third inch in diameter, but a deer's much larger ear allows more sound waves to be picked up and funneled.

"Another advantage that deer have is that their range of hearing is much wider than humans'. Most human adults can hear frequencies in the range of 40 to 16,000 cycles per second, with some people, especially children, hearing both lower and higher frequencies than is normal.

"I know that deer can hear frequencies as high as 30,000 cycles and perhaps beyond. I often use a 'silent' dog whistle while doing photography, to get a deer's attention and cause it to look at me alertly. These devices have been machine tested at 30,000 cycles, and although humans can't hear them, dogs and deer respond readily."

I've observed that whitetails have the ability to filter out certain non-threatening sounds to

*During the seeking and chasing phase of the rut, bucks actively pursue all does in their area in an attempt to find one to breed. By trapping the scent from a doe's urine in their nose, and Flehmening, a buck can tell which doe is in or coming into estrus.*

which they are accustomed. Sounds like acorns and apples dropping, leaves lightly rustling on tree branches, and traffic along a nearby highway are all sounds deer are used to. However, when high winds cause tree branches to crash together or the weight of a human's foot causes a twig to snap, deer become skittish very quickly.

***Taste:*** Of all the whitetail's senses, its ability to taste is probably the weakest. Research has shown there are over 500 natural plants that deer will eat. Through the years, I've noticed deer decide what they will eat by smelling food before tasting it.

Through the combination of smelling and

*Whitetails have an incredible craving for foods high in sugar. Consequently, they gravitate to orchards and other fruit-producing sources.*

then tasting, whitetails determine which plants and browse they prefer. However, not all deer like the same foods. In 2001, I teamed up on an extensive nutritional research project with North Country Whitetails and Cornell University. The goal was to determine the nutritional levels of preferred and non-preferred leaves and browse.

We found that most deer at my research facility preferred and disliked the same species. However, a couple of the deer in the project loved American beech browse. This is considered a non-preferred food for the whitetail, in spite of the fact that it is higher in crude protein than many other preferred species of browse. Although most of the deer paid little attention to the American beech throughout the study, it was

obvious that its taste was attractive to two of them. This resembled the differences in taste that exist among many humans.

**Touch:** The sense of touch is extremely important to the whitetail. The way a doe washes and cleans her newborn fawn and the manner in which a buck and doe groom and rub each other during the breeding process illustrate the importance of touching in the whitetail's communication system.

Grooming is a very important social behavior that is carried out between virtually all combinations of deer—does and fawns, does and does, does and bucks, and bucks and bucks. Through touching, licking and nuzzling, deer show their affection toward each other.

When a doe grooms her newborn fawn, she leaves saliva on it, which helps the fawn to imprint on the doe. When grooming takes place between bucks, the lower buck in the dominance hierarchy usually, but not always, initiates it. Such grooming sessions often last between 2 and 10 minutes before one of the bucks breaks off the grooming by leaving the area, bedding, or feeding.

During the breeding phase of the rut, a buck will touch a doe in an effort to stimulate her. This foreplay, which occurs in the form of mutual grooming or a buck licking the doe's genital area, helps to speed up the breeding process.

Forehead Gland

Preorbital Gland

Nasal Gland

Tarsal Gland

Metatarsal Gland

# Glands

The various glands on a whitetail's body play a major role in its behavioral tendencies. Deer use their sense of smell to interpret the odors given off by the forehead, preorbital, nasal, tarsal, metatarsal and interdigital glands. Each of these glands plays a significant role in the way whitetails communicate and are attracted to each other.

*Forehead gland:* Located on a deer's forehead (between the eyes and antler burrs on a buck), the forehead gland is used by a buck when he rubs his forehead on trees, branches, and brush. It's a way for each animal to leave his own distinct odor on rubs and licking branches. Researchers believe this odor works as a rutting stimulant for both bucks and does.

As September inches toward November, rubbing behavior increases in whitetail country. When a buck makes a rub, he lays down a layer of odors from his forehead, nasal and preorbital glands.

*Preorbital and nasal glands:* Located just below the inner corner of the eye, the preorbital gland is primarily a tear duct. However, it also plays a significant role in the scrape-making process. When a whitetail buck makes a scrape, he rubs his preorbital gland on the overhanging branch to leave as much scent as possible. A buck will also rub his preorbital gland on brush, rubbing sticks, and other types of vegetation in order to deposit scent. Though seldom discussed, the nasal gland is also important to the whitetail's ability to leave scent. In the process of making a rub, a buck will often pause between rubbing his antlers and forehead gland and actually smell the tree and rub his wet nose on it. By touching his nose to the rub, a buck leaves even more scent to inform other deer of his presence.

*Tarsal gland:* For a variety of reasons, the tarsal gland is the most common gland known to whitetail hunters. It's by far the strongest-smelling gland on a deer's body. Tarsal glands are located on the insides of whitetails' hind legs. The odor emitted by them is used as an olfactory signal that deer use to identify each other.

These glands play a big part in a buck's behavior during the rut. Throughout the year, a buck's tarsal glands are constantly changing. For most of the year, they are cream to light brown in color. As October inches toward November in the North, whitetail bucks become more and more active as they search for estrous does. In the process of my photography, I've observed that the hair on a buck's tarsal glands becomes darker between October 25 and November 10 with tarsal glands on dominant bucks frequently appearing chocolate brown or black in color.

Throughout the year, a buck will exhibit a behavior known as rub-urination. However, during November, this will become more frequent. During the rut, a buck will stand in a scrape with his hind legs together, allowing urine to pass over his tarsal glands before it falls into the scrape. The combination of tarsal scent and urine creates a strong odor in the scrape and works as a powerful attractant for rutting bucks and does.

**Metatarsal gland:** Located within a white tuft of hair on the outside of the hind leg just above the dewclaw, the metatarsal gland is a mystery to both hunters and researchers. It has long been felt that this gland emits a pheromone that alarms whitetails.

**Interdigital gland:** If you were to separate the toes of a whitetail, you'd find an opening between them, almost resembling a small tunnel. The interdigital gland is located within this opening. This gland emits a yellow waxy

*Researchers have shown that there are over 500 natural plants that deer will eat. They love leaves and will consume a high volume of them throughout the year.*

substance that resembles human earwax. Like fingerprints in humans, its excretion is never the same from one deer to another. The odor it leaves behind allows deer to trail each other in the woods.

## Communication

Unless you know the language, it's tough to know the creature. This applies to both people and wild animals.

**Vocalization:** Whitetails are no different from other animals in that they are social creatures. Throughout their lives, they communicate with each other using a variety of bleats, grunts and snorts. For the first 6 months of life, fawns bleat and mew to their mothers. Adult

*Hierarchy in the buck population is ongoing among its members. In this photo, a yearling buck attempts to socialize with a mature buck.*

out series of grunts), and contact call (which is a shorter grunt than a tending grunt).

Having spent a tremendous amount of time around whitetails during the last 15 years, I feel there may be sounds not specifically identified in the University of Georgia study that are actually more common at certain times of year than those mentioned above. An example is a long, drawn-out grunt often made by a frustrated buck when he is courting an estrous doe and is being harassed by other bucks. I've heard this grunt last for over a minute and found it to be a very common vocalization used by rutting bucks as they interact with estrous does and competing males. Another very common sound is what I call a grunt-wheeze. This is an aggressive grunt followed by a drawn-out wheeze that is often made by a dominant buck and is directed at subordinate bucks. I often incorporate this vocalization into calling techniques when photographing and hunting. It's a great call to use when attempting to bring rut-crazed bucks close to your blind or stand.

I've also observed that each deer has a slightly different way of vocalizing. No two deer sound exactly alike. However, of the hundreds of deer I've been around, nearly all sounded very similar when making the common snort, snort-wheeze, low grunt, bleat, and the call I refer to as the grunt-wheeze.

***Body language:*** Few things get a deer's attention faster than the aggressive body

bucks and does also communicate with each other by grunting and bleating. And, of course, whitetails snort to alert each other of danger.

Several notable research projects have investigated the various aspects of whitetail vocalization. Of these, a study conducted at the University of Georgia in 1988 by Atkeson, Marchinton and Miller is perhaps the most respected. In this project, the researchers recorded approximately 400 different whitetail vocalizations. After the initial recording process was complete, 90 common sounds were identified. From there, the researchers were able to determine the 12 calls whitetails make most often. These 12 vocalizations include the snort, bawl, low grunt, grunt-snort, grunt-snort-wheeze, maternal grunt, mew, bleat, nursing whine, Flehman sniff, tending grunt (which is a drawn-

*During the rut's chase phase, bucks aggressively seek out does. Sometimes the process can be humorous. This doe was attempting to flee this buck, but for some reason stopped abruptly, causing the buck to run into her from behind.*

language of another buck or doe. All deer have a way of getting their message across without saying a "word." They do it with the subtle drop of an ear, a cock of the head, or by flexing their erector pili muscles so that their hair bristles up, making them look like an irritated porcupine. Simply put, the way deer communicate with their bodies is fascinating.

The whitetail gets its name from the white hair on the underside of its tail. When alarmed, a deer will often raise its tail and flare it out. The tail-flare allows whitetails to alert each other of possible danger. On mature deer, this makes the tail nearly 12 inches wide. In the process of flaring the tail, the erector pili muscles reverse the rump hair so that the entire deer is white when observed from the rear. Often when they

are in this position, deer will strut and wave their tails back and forth, giving the appearance that they are trying to alert all deer that something is wrong.

The "hard stare" is a rather common form of body language used by both dominant bucks and does. When a doe exhibits this behavior, she usually holds her head high and lays her ears back, letting her adversary know rather emphatically she means business. The final stage of a doe's hard stare comes in the form of her flailing at her adversary with her hoofs. A doe often will use the hard stare if a buck comes too close to her fawns or if she feels the need to keep another deer away from her food.

When bucks exhibit the hard stare, they do so to intimidate rivals and subordinate bucks. However, their technique is different from that of the does. A buck will pull his ears back and then approach his rival in a circular fashion. While on approach, a buck often will bristle his hair, slide or shuffle his feet, walk with a stiff-legged gait, and hold his head low and tucked so that his antlers are projected forward. In addition, his eyes generally have an aggressive appearance and he'll frequently use grunts and grunt-wheezes. When bucks exhibit such behavior toward each other, incredible fights can occur if neither animal backs down.

Aggressive pawing is a behavior that takes place when one buck approaches another and begins pawing the ground in an aggressive manner. Each fall I witness this numerous times when a mature free-ranging buck approaches one of the bucks on the inside of my research facility. The wild buck will come within a few feet of the high fence and proceed to drop his ears, bristle his coat, and feverishly paw the ground.

In 1989, while hunting the brush country of south Texas, I watched two large mature bucks walk to within 30 yards of each other and begin to aggressively paw the ground. It was a very dry year, and both bucks made small dust plumes as they tried to out-paw each other. After a minute or so, they stopped and moved closer. The fight that followed was incredible. It lasted less than a minute, but while they brawled in the brush, several other bucks emerged from the surrounding cover to check out the fight.

Aggressive rubbing and scraping is the final behavior worth noting. When the hot-to-trot breeding phase of the rut is occurring and several bucks are vying for the same doe, there can be a lot of competition for breeding rights. Such a scenario creates the ultimate breeding party. To keep subordinate bucks at bay, a dominant buck will often take out his frustration and show his superiority by aggressively rubbing and, ultimately, trashing nearby brush. Such outbursts can be quite impressive, and they usually are more than enough to keep lesser bucks from attempting to take the doe from him. In addition, the dominant buck often will feverishly work a low-hanging branch and paw the ground underneath it as a way to demonstrate his aggression and dominance.

*Even in late winter, fighting may occur when bucks strive for dominance. I took this photo in late January, and for a few moments, the fight resembled a November brawl.*

# CHAPTER 16

# In Search of the Future

The history of wildlife management in America is fascinating. When the Europeans arrived on our shores, they found a continent teeming with wildlife. Chief among the animal species was the white-tailed deer. Because of the whitetail's abundance and its importance to Native Americans, it was the king of North American wildlife. Nearly 400 years have passed since the Pilgrims landed at Plymouth, and the whitetail continues to hold this position.

Some would say that the whitetail's status among sportsmen and nature lovers has never been stronger. Certainly the white-tailed deer population is greater than at any time in recorded history. For those who love to watch deer, this is good. However, the consequences of overpopulation have created a host of problems that impact our environment's present and future.

My association with the whitetail goes back to my childhood in rural western New York in the 1950s. As I reflect back to my youth, I feel blessed to have grown up in the country. Farm life could be hard, but being surrounded by nature had a way of easing the strain. Roaming the wild haunts of my parents' farm was always special. In many ways, it gave me a foundation for the values that guide me today. Part of this foundation was a sound work ethic and a keen understanding of the word stewardship.

The farming community where I lived was made up of rugged individuals who toiled in the fields from sunup to sundown. There weren't too many forms of recreation, but one of the biggest was deer hunting in the fall. The farmers in the area loved the sight of whitetails, but they also realized the deer needed to be harvested just like corn, alfalfa and potatoes. Because of the damage deer were capable of inflicting on crops, the need to keep the herd in balance with the land's carrying capacity was well understood. This philosophy was viewed as a basic premise of being good stewards of the land. Unfortunately, as we ease into the 21st century, the notion of managing the deer herd through hunting has met resistance in many parts of America.

## Population Explosion

When the Europeans arrived, it's estimated that North America was home to 20 million white-tailed deer. Due to habitat loss, open seasons and market hunting, the population plummeted to about 500,000 by the early 1900s. A cry went out from sportsmen and statesmen, resulting in the end of deer hunting in many regions.

To allow the population to recover, deer were not hunted for more than 30 years in some parts of the country. As a result, the whitetail staged an incredible comeback. This recovery was one of the greatest wildlife management feats of the last century, and today it is estimated that the whitetail population in America is over 30 million. Many biologists believe this number is over 10-15 million more than the range can support. With habitat being destroyed at a record rate, it is clear that something must be done to curb the expansion of the whitetail population. I believe that if biologists could manage deer herds in a scientific manner, rather than have their plans stifled politically, whitetail numbers could be controlled very efficiently. Unfortunately, their proposals are often modified by our political system.

Instead of viewing the whitetail population as a renewable resource, certain groups within our society have promoted the idea that it is morally wrong to harvest deer. As a result, politicians have faced considerable pressure to curb or eliminate hunting, which continues to be the only efficient way to control excess deer

*As the whitetail population continues to explode in urban America, authorities will be challenged to come up with ways to control deer numbers.*

*Next to exploding populations, the inability of hunters to access land will become more and more of a problem in controlling deer populations in the future.*

*When deer populations exceed a range's carrying capacity, the natural habitat quickly suffers. In many parts of America, habitat damage from overbrowsing has become so severe that it will take decades to recover.*

populations. In addition to mismanagement, environmental factors, societal changes and emerging diseases also threaten the future of the whitetail in North America.

## Societal Shift

Society began to change at an increasing rate after World War II. Prior to 1950, America was predominately an agrarian society. A majority of Americans lived in rural areas and made their living tending the soil. In the last 50 years, this has changed and most people now live within 50 miles of America's major cities and make their living in areas other than agriculture. Because of

this shift, the average American's view of the whitetail has changed considerably.

Today far fewer people understand the importance of controlling deer numbers through hunting. When I was a kid, hunter education was actually taught in the public school I attended. Today, the mere mention of guns and hunting receives a negative reaction in many schools.

For the last 40 years, the anti-hunting movement has been gaining momentum. In the beginning, its message was relatively faint, but today it is deafening. Much of the anti-hunting agenda has been conveyed through the public school system. A few years ago I did an article for

*Deer and Deer Hunting* magazine that focused on the declining number of hunters. Part of my research looked into the hunting-related literature that was available to public school teachers. I was surprised to find that anti-hunting literature outnumbered pro-hunting material 4-to-1. It's tough to teach kids the importance of managing wildlife populations when they are taught (for the most part) that hunting is cruel and barbaric.

## Hunter Decline

A byproduct of society's shift from an agrarian to an urban setting has been a decline in the number of deer hunters entering the woods each fall. There are several reasons for this. Dysfunctional families, peer pressure, too many competing activities, poor recruitment of hunters, and a lack of places to hunt are just a few things that have contributed to a drop in the hunting population.

The average age of deer hunters in America is now 46 years, up nearly 10 years from a decade ago. Less than 10 years ago, my home state of New York had over 700,000 deer hunters. It's projected that within the next decade, this number will dip below 500,000.

Without the recruitment of younger hunters, it will be difficult to attain the deer harvest required to keep whitetail herds in line with the range's carrying capacity. Introducing a child to the deer hunting experience requires a considerable commitment. It involves taking a kid to the woods at an early age on a repeated basis, usually for short periods of time. Sadly, less of this is occurring today. Without a hunter development program, the mechanism for controlling deer populations is threatened.

## Habitat/Access Loss

Of all the challenges facing whitetails today, the loss of habitat may be the greatest. Every deer requires approximately 1½ tons of food per year to survive. Of this, roughly half should come from

*This is a classic example of what happens when there are too many deer. Everything visible in this photo was clear-cut five years ago. The habitat on the right has been high-fenced, so deer cannot browse. On the left, the deer have eaten everything in sight.*

natural sources. Unfortunately, most of America's whitetail herds are nearing or exceeding their environment's carrying capacity. As a result, natural habitat is being destroyed at a record pace. The northeastern part of the United States has been experiencing habitat degradation for the last two decades. Much of this region can handle 20-35 deer per square mile. In reality, it is bursting at its seams with 70 or more deer per square mile in many areas. If it weren't for farm crops, this region's deer population would have crashed by now.

Unfortunately, less and less land is being use for farming. When I was growing up in the '50s and '60s, about 70 percent of western New York State was farmland, and most of the balance was forested. Today the exact opposite is true. Some might see this as good, but in reality the deer population in most areas has been so high for so long that regeneration in the forest is nearly impossible. The whitetail has literally eaten itself out of house and home.

Pennsylvania, New York, New Jersey and other states have worked hard to come up with ways to control their exploding whitetail

*Controlling doe numbers will be key as we look to the future. Without ample antlerless harvests, the natural habitat will continue to decline in quality.*

*Controlling whitetail numbers through hunting is the only proven way to control deer numbers.*

populations. Programs designed to harvest more antlerless deer like Earn-A-Buck, Deer Management Assistance Permits (DMAP), and others have gone a long way toward curbing the population explosion. All are excellent, but hunters must have access to land for the programs to be most effective.

Inadequate access to hunting land is a problem that has been emerging for the last 10-20 years. Each year more and more land is being posted and put off-limits to hunting. This is perhaps the greatest threat to hunting and deer management. If hunters cannot get on the land to harvest the excess deer, it doesn't matter how many antlerless permits are available.

## Disease

When too many deer inhabit an area, it's only a matter of time before the health of the herd declines. This often occurs through disease. In recent years, the threat of Chronic Wasting Disease (CWD) in whitetails has become a real concern among deer experts. At this time, no one knows the origin of CWD. However, everyone agrees that it represents a serious problem for the whitetail and the deer hunting movement.

Nearly all experts agree that a reduction of deer populations can help to curb CWD and other diseases. For the white-tailed deer to thrive in the future, populations must be controlled.

# The Hunter's Role in Sound Management

Regardless of what the critics say, hunting is the only sound way to manage today's whitetail numbers. It is the most cost effective, humane and scientific way known to control the deer population.

Critics claim that hunting is cruel and inhumane. However, I've lived my whole life around whitetails, and I'm convinced that hunting is very humane relative to the alternatives.

To me the most inhumane way to manage whitetails is to let them overpopulate an area and then suffer from disease and lack of food. Few have seen the way predators like wolves, coyotes and domestic dogs hunt and kill whitetails. I have, and believe me, it's hard to imagine a more inhumane and cruel death. They sometimes take hours to kill a deer, whereas a hunter's bullet or arrow can take seconds. Hunting is by far the most ethical way to manage the deer population.

In addition to hunting being the most efficient way to control deer numbers, it should be pointed out that hunters make a considerable contribution to the economy. According to the National Shooting Sports Foundation, hunters pump almost $30 billion into the U.S. economy each year, supporting more than 986,000 jobs. For every 25 hunters, enough economic activity is generated to create one job. For every taxpayer dollar invested in wildlife conservation, sportsmen contribute $12. Through over 10,000 private groups and organizations (such as Whitetails Unlimited, Ducks Unlimited,

National Wild Turkey Federation, Rocky Mountain Elk Foundation and others), sportsmen contribute an additional $300 million each year to wildlife conservation activities. The bottom line is that wildlife would be in dire trouble without the financial support of the hunting community.

## Quality Deer Management

Despite the negative impacts of excess populations, societal change, declining hunter numbers, shrinking access and disease, the whitetail's future does have a silver lining. The outlook is reasonably bright because more and more hunters and landowners are addressing the problems and becoming educated on what is required for the deer population to thrive. The quality deer management (QDM) movement is expanding in virtually every corner of the whitetail's range.

In a nutshell, QDM is a form of deer management that seeks quality in each segment of the deer population—bucks, does, and fawns. Yearling and 2-year-old bucks are protected to increase the number of mature males, and the harvest of does is emphasized in order to control the adult-doe-to-antlered buck ratio. In addition, QDM strives to keep deer habitat at a high level. It also improves landowner relations and creates quality hunters. The end result is a quality deer herd and better habitat, which benefits nature lovers and hunters alike, not to mention the deer.

Quality deer management will certainly play a major role in the way that whitetails are managed in the future. Ten years ago, QDM could have been compared to a faint echo in the

*As this century unfolds, there are many unanswered questions concerning the whitetail. However, with proper planning and management, this magnificent animal can thrive and survive.*

wilderness. Outside of Texas and portions of the Southeast, it received very little serious consideration. In little more than a decade, the concept has exploded. This has occurred because QDM is a common sense, biologically-sound management method.

The direction of QDM is best summed up by Brian Murphy, executive director of the Quality Deer Management Association: "With increasing challenges facing the future of deer hunting and management, such as increasing deer populations, declining hunter numbers and continued threats from animal-rights and gun-control groups, the QDMA is increasingly well-equipped to face these and other challenges. Clearly, QDM has arrived and will be the dominant management strategy as we progress through the 21st century."

Additional information about the Quality Deer Management Association is available on the organization's website, www.qdma.com.

## Venison Donation

Bringing whitetail numbers in line with the range's carrying capacity means that more deer must be harvested. Consequently, hunters and deer managers must find additional ways to make use of the increased harvest. After all, a hunting family can only eat so much venison. In the past few years, an organization called Farmers and Hunters Feeding the Hungry (FHFH) has established a sizable network that helps hunters donate excess venison to needy families, food banks, and soup kitchens. The success of FHFH and a similar program in my home state of New York known as the Venison Donation Coalition has been overwhelming. Such programs are an ideal complement to quality deer management and provide sportsmen with an opportunity to give back to the community. For information on FHFH, call (301) 739-3000 or visit www.fhfh.org.

Because of the efforts of sportsmen involved in organizations like QDMA and FHFH, the whitetail's future remains bright in spite of the problems it faces. It is a resourceful and resilient animal, and with a little help from man, it will continue to thrive.

# CHAPTER 17

# Capturing the Memories

I have to be honest with you, whenever I pick up a magazine or book, the first thing I do is flip through the pages to examine the photos. If nothing catches my eye, I move on. But if a photo grabs my attention, I might spend a considerable amount of time surveying the rest of the book. Though this may sound odd, it really isn't. Scientists tell us that learning is 80 percent visual, and humans respond more quickly to visual stimuli than anything else. Without the images captured by wildlife photographers, our understanding of the natural world would be considerably less.

Most who make their living as nature photographers say they have the best job in the world. I definitely feel this way, but that doesn't mean it's an easy profession. Believe me, it can be very disheartening at times if you don't know what you are doing.

The essence of wildlife photography was summed up best by my good friend and master whitetail photographer Mike Biggs, who said, "Wildlife photography consists of a series of repeated attempts by a crazed individual to obtain impossible photos of unpredictable subjects performing unlikely behaviors under outrageous circumstances." Though a bit humorous, this is, in a nutshell, what whitetail photography is all about.

Due to the whitetail's unpredictable nature, it is impossible to always be successful as a deer photographer. However, a heavy dose of persistence, knowledge of the animal, and the right equipment make it possible to capture great images of America's favorite big game animal.

It's safe to say that wildlife photography has added greater meaning to my life. My quest to get one more photo has often kept me in the woods when I should have called it a day. Through nature photography, I've come to truly appreciate God's incredible creation. I wholeheartedly believe that my mission in life is to photograph the wonders of God's handiwork and share them with others. In large part, this is why I do what I do. The other part is that I love it so much.

## Roots and Tools

While growing up on a potato farm in western New York, I filled my early years with hunting and trapping. When I was 20 and in the U.S. Air Force, I spent a year in Vietnam. While there, I was introduced to the 35mm camera. My motive for buying the camera and assorted telephoto lenses was the opportunity to hunt deer with film when they couldn't be hunted with a bow or gun. After being discharged from the service in 1970, I began to seriously photograph deer and other wildlife. As I soon discovered, the beauty of hunting with a camera is that the season lasts all year and there are no bag limits.

I shoot Nikon cameras and lenses. Presently, I rely heavily on five lenses: a 20-35mm f2.8, a 35-70mm f2.8, an 80-200mm f2.8 AF-S, a 500mm f4.0 AF-S, and a 200-400mm f4.0 ED zoom. These lenses are extremely sharp (and expensive!) and allow me to photograph when the light is less than adequate. I always try to use the 80-200mm zoom mounted on a tripod or gunstock, though I will shoot it off-hand if lighting permits. The 500mm and the 200-400mm zoom are fairly heavy and are always used

*To enhance whitetail photos, try to develop an eye for composition. Rather than tight portraits, add the environment and place the animal off-center.*

with a tripod to ensure that the pictures are as sharp as possible.

The color film I use changes with technology. For years I primarily shot Kodachrome 64, which I consider to be one of the best films ever made. Since the "film wars" heated up, film quality has continuously improved; this has led me to shoot whatever film I perceive as the best at any given time. I presently use three color slide films for the bulk of my photography: Fuji Velvia (ASA 50) for scenics, Fuji 100 Sensia (ASA 100) for animals, and Fuji 400F Provia (ASA 400) for low-light situations.

I use Fuji Velvia for scenics because it's one of the sharpest films made and its colors are incredible. I shoot it at its ASA rating of 50. Fuji Sensia 100 is nearly as sharp as Velvia, and I shoot it at its ASA rating of 100. Fuji 400F Provia is my fast-speed film, and I shoot it at its ASA rating of 400. I like to call it "magic film." It is relatively new and performs incredibly. I've never used a fast speed film quite like it. It is sharp and holds colors well, and it is excellent in overcast conditions. The only downside is its cost.

As far as film is concerned, it's important to remember a couple things. First, always shoot slide film. In most cases, better prints can be made from slides than with print film. Slides are also easier to scan and are more easily marketed to publishers. Second, slower ASA films will be sharper and have better colors. Unfortunately, everything is a trade-off, and using slow-speed film usually means shooting off a tripod.

*To capture snow movement, use a shutter speed of 125 or less. Anything faster will freeze the flakes. Movement gives the photo a sense of mood, mystique and action.*

## Equipment

As I write this, the world of photography is rapidly changing. The digital movement has created a big groundswell, and it looks like film will soon be a thing of the past. Obviously, cameras are vastly different than when I began photographing in the late '60s. Except for the light meter, my first 35mm was completely manual. Today, most of my cameras have all the "bells and whistles" and are truly state-of-the-art. They are capable of autofocus, can advance the film at nearly six frames per second, offer several programming modes, and have outstanding meter systems. With such incredible technology, it's no wonder many amateurs are able to get the outstanding photos they do.

The nature of whitetail photography makes 35mm the format of choice. Whenever someone asks me about what camera I'd recommend for photographing deer, I ask them how much money they are willing to spend and if they want to use film or digital. Today's cameras are not cheap. The more features they have, the more costly they are. For the novice to serious amateur, I recommend a medium-priced 35mm camera body and a zoom lens in the 35-70mm range. This lens has a magnification of wide angle to about 1¼ power and is excellent for scenics (note that the lens' magnification can be calculated by dividing 50 into the lens' millimeter).

In order to start photographing deer, a zoom lens in the 80-200mm range is essential. Also, it's best to get the lowest "f" setting you can afford. I have three 80-200mm lenses that are f2.8, and they allow me to photograph in dim light (the smaller the "f" number, the less light required to take a picture). Also, most of today's telephoto lenses offer teleconverters that are matched to

*Always be ready for action. If you think there is the possibility of action, make sure your camera's shutter speed will go off at over a 500th of a second.*

the lens. A 1.4 teleconverter only loses 1 "f" stop of light and will make an 80-200mm f2.8 lens into a 110-280mm f4.0 lens. People often think most deer photos are taken with long lenses. Though many are, the 80-200mm is my workhorse lens and a favorite when it comes to shooting whitetails.

For the person serious about photographing deer, a 300mm, or better yet a 400mm or 500mm, is a must if you want to reach the hard-to-approach animals. A 300mm (6 power), 400mm (8 power), or 500mm (10 power) will allow you to fill the frame with an animal without taking the risk of spooking it. Longer lenses also are able

*Photography is light. Success hinges on how well you handle each lighting situation. Remember that the best sunlit photos will come during the two hours either side of darkness.*

*Whenever photographing wildlife, work to do so at the animal's eye level. Also, be sure to focus on the eye as it is the center of attraction.*

to blur out the background, which is aesthetically pleasing when doing portrait photography.

In most instances, the deer images that grace the covers of major magazines are taken with 300-600mm lenses. The downsides of these lenses are their weight and cost. The weight of most requires the use of a tripod. And the sticker price on these models can make a person cry or tremble, depending on his or her frame of mind. At today's prices, one can expect to pay anywhere from $1000 for a long telephoto to over $6000 for a top-of-the-line model. As with the other lenses, the lower the "f" setting, the better your chances of photographing in dim light. Lenses with lower "f" settings will also be the most expensive.

A sturdy tripod is one of the last pieces of equipment required to get into deer photography. Even though it's the last piece of equipment I mention, don't try to cut corners in this area, as the quality of your photos depends on how steady the camera is when you are shooting. To lighten the load, I use carbon tripods. My lightweight model is a Gitzo G1228. My serious tripod—the one I use for my long lenses—is a Gitzo G1325. Both tripods sport an ARCA ball head.

Though it isn't as steady as a tripod, a shoulder stock (or gunstock) can help to create sharp photos when you need to be mobile. Both BushHawk and Rue Enterprises market excellent shoulder stocks.

One piece of equipment that isn't necessary but is nice to have for whitetail photography is a portable blind. You can either make your own or purchase one of many on the market. Dollar for dollar, Rue Enterprises' Ultimate Photo Blind (www.Rue.com) is hard to beat. It is lightweight and can be put in place in less than a minute. I've spent countless hours in this blind and have taken some great photos while using it.

## Making the Photo

Mark Twain once said, "You can't depend on your eyes if your imagination is out of focus." Though this quote wasn't directed at photography, it could have been. Whenever I conduct photography seminars I emphasize to attendees that their goal should be to "make photos," not "take photos." There is a vast difference between the two. Rather than reacting spontaneously, think creatively when practicing the art of nature photography.

When I first began photographing deer, I *took* photos. In the early 70s, I was more intent on just getting the deer in the frame than thinking about composition, depth of field or lighting. All these aspects of photography take time to develop, but with a little knowledge, the learning curve can be shortened.

Light is the key to nature photography, and

*For the best sunlit photos, try positioning the animal so that it is either back lit or side lit.*

*Action photos don't just happen. Stopping running whitetails in midjump requires a shutter speed of 1000.*

whenever possible, I try to position the deer so they will not be in direct sunlight. If I have a choice, I like to cross-light or back-light my subject. This kind of lighting makes for more dramatic photos; getting it often requires forethought and planning.

Like lighting, the composition of a photo is essential to its appeal. When composing whitetail shots, or photos of any wildlife for that matter, I try to think how the subject will look best. Therefore, I often put the subject off center in the picture so it becomes a part of the scene. In order to enhance the photo's composition, I'll try to find a tree or some other object to frame the animal. This technique often makes photos much more appealing from an artistic standpoint. To

put it another way, I try to have my photos tell a story. This is not to say that I don't like to take tight portraits, because I do. However, I try to get artistic whenever the opportunity presents itself.

When taking portraits of animals, I always focus on the subject's eyes. The eye is the center of attention and reveals the soul and character of the subject. In addition, the glint of the eye adds life to the photo. I also like to take pictures from the subject's eye level. If the subject is a fawn lying on the forest floor, I photograph on my belly.

My best photos usually occur when I go back to a location several times. During the course of photographing, I constantly survey the scene to see which location will provide the best photo

*If water is present, try to get the animal reflected in the photo; doing so will greatly enhance the quality of the photo.*

opportunities when the sun shines. Because baiting is usually allowed where I photograph, I preplan where I'll place the bait to get deer in the right position for the photos I want.

Baiting can be done in many forms, and it's wise to find out what is legal where you live. Due to recent deer diseases like Chronic Wasting, baiting has been banned in some areas. I learned a long time ago that the fastest way to a whitetail is through its stomach. As a result, I use apples and corn to lure deer within camera range. I also use one other device, a deer decoy.

During autumn, white-tailed bucks respond well to a doe or buck decoy. This is especially true during the mating season. I've used decoys extensively and had some incredible experiences with them. If you want to try "deercoying," it's important that a buck be able to spot the decoy, so placing it in an open area is essential. Also, make sure the decoy is anchored to the ground. When a buck approaches a decoy, he often becomes aggressive and if the fake deer isn't anchored, it will probably get knocked over, ending the shoot. A word of caution is in order, however. Never use a decoy where hunting is permitted. Today's decoys are works of art and appear very authentic. As a result, from a distance, hunters will seldom be able to tell the difference between a decoy and the real thing. So always keep safety in mind.

Perhaps the greatest challenge in nature photography is capturing action. Things can occur fast in the wild, and getting it right doesn't just happen. In order to stop fast movement, you need to shoot a shutter speed of at least a 500th of a second, or 1000th of a second if you have enough light. Of course, there will be times when you want to show action by blurring the movement. Creating a sense of motion can be accomplished by shooting at a shutter speed of a 15th of a second or slower. The slower the shutter speed, the greater the blur.

## Where to Make the Photos

Making good deer photos is much easier now than when I broke into the photography business. With urbanization, zoning laws that prohibit hunting, and more and more people raising whitetails, there are numerous opportunities to photograph deer. The trick to all of this is finding out where the locations exist. A good place to start is your state's department of natural resources, which should be able to provide you with a list of individuals who raise deer. Once this has been done, contact some of the farmers on the list to find out if photography is possible at their facilities. In addition, local conservation officers or deer biologists should be contacted to find out if any landowners in your area are feeding deer.

I do a great deal of whitetail photography on our farm and have many blind locations right on our "back 40." When I first began, I relied on photographing in deer wintering areas. Though I still do this, I also photograph on big estates, ranches, national parks (like Smoky Mountain National Park, where deer are used to people), and around metropolitan areas where hunting is limited or prohibited. These locations can be excellent for photography, though cropping cars and houses out of the pictures is sometimes a challenge.

*Using a decoy can improve one's chance of luring a buck within camera range. To improve the situation, try adding motion to the decoy.*

# References

**Books:**

*Amazing Whitetails*, Mike Biggs, T.P.W., Inc.

*Deer*, edited by Gerlach, Atwater, Schnell, Stackpole Books.

*Grow 'em Right*, Neil and Craig Dougherty, www.NorthCountry Whitetails.com

*Hunting Whitetails by the Moon*, Charles J. Alsheimer, Krause Publications, www.CharlesAlsheimer.com

*Leonard Lee Rue III's Way of the Whitetail*, Dr. Leonard Lee Rue III, Voyageur Press.

*Producing Quality Whitetails*, Al Brothers and Murphy E. Ray, Jr., Texas Wildlife Association.

*Quality Deer Management: The Basics and Beyond*, Charles J. Alsheimer, Krause Publications, www.CharlesAlsheimer.com

*Quality Whitetails*, edited by Karl V. Miller and R. Larry Marchinton, Stackpole Books.

*The Whitetail Chronicles*, Mike Biggs, T.P.W., Inc.

*Understanding Whitetails*, Dr. Dave Samuel, Cowles Creative Publishing.

*Whitetail: Behavior Through the Seasons*, Charles J. Alsheimer, Krause Publications, www.CharlesAlsheimer.com

*Whitetail Autumn*, John J. Ozoga, Willow Creek Press.

*Whitetail Country*, John J. Ozoga, Willow Creek Press.

*Whitetail Intrigue*, John J. Ozoga, Krause Publications.

*Whitetail Monarchs*, George Barnett, Willow Creek Press.

*Whitetail Spring*, John J. Ozoga, Willow Creek Press.

*Whitetail Summer*, John J. Ozoga, Willow Creek Press.

*Whitetail Winter*, John J. Ozoga, Willow Creek Press.

*White-tailed Deer—Ecology and Management*, edited by Lowell K. Halls, Stackpole Books.

*Whitetails: Behavior, Ecology, Conservation*, Erwin Bauer, Voyageur Press.

*Whitetails in Action*, Mike Biggs, T.P.W., Inc.

*25 Years of Deer and Deer Hunting*, edited by Daniel E. Schmidt, Krause Publications.

**Periodicals:**

*Deer and Deer Hunting* magazine, Krause Publications, 700 E. State St., Iola, WI 54990.

*Quality Whitetails*, Official Publication of the Quality Deer Management Association.

*Whitetail News*, Official Publication of the Whitetail Institute of North America.

**Organizations:**

Farmers and Hunters Feeding the Hungry
216 North Cleveland Ave.
Hagerstown, MD 21740
301-739-3000
www.FHFH.org

North Country Whitetails
PO Box 925
Fairport, NY 14450
585-388-6990
www.NorthCountryWhitetails.com

Quality Deer Management Association
P.O. Box 227
Watkinsville, GA 30677
800-209-3337
www.QDMA.com

Whitetail Institute of North America
Route 1, Box 3006
Pintlala, AL 36043
334-281-3006
www.DeerNutrition.com

# Index